PRAISE FOR *15 MINUTE MEALS*

"Written in her accessible and welcoming tone, Ali Rosen has created a book full of flavorful and delicious dishes that will actually get dinner on the table in 15 minutes. The recipes are cleverly organized in a time-saving way, plus sprinkled throughout are smart shortcuts, tips on maximizing flavor, and sourcing quick-cooking cuts of meat, fish and vegetables. *15 Minute Meals* will surely be a weeknight savior for busy home cooks."

—Yasmin Fahr, *New York Times* contributor and author of *What's for Dinner and Keeping It Simple*

"Ali Rosen's *15 Minute Meals* is undeniably prescient, timely, and delicious. We all need quick meal recipes that feel like dinner, not like silly social media video hacks. I don't know about you, but as a single dad who is always on the move, I found this book to be a life preserver of the highest order. From Bucatini a l'Amtriciania-ish to the brilliance of Ground Chicken Piccata, this is the weeknight meals collection that we should be celebrating, and cooking from."

—Andrew Zimmern, Emmy and James Beard Award-winning TV host, chef and writer

"If anyone can convince me that so many excellent dishes can be accomplished in 15 minutes, it's Ali! Each recipe comes with a pinch of honesty and humor, and a realistic approach to getting maximum flavor in minimal time through smart ingredients and comfort in your kitchen. If all of these dishes can be achieved in 15 minutes, imagine what else we can all accomplish with the time we'll save!"

—Adrienne Cheatham, James Beard Nominated chef, author, and television personality

"Ali Rosen's joyful new cookbook *15 Minutes Meals* offers inventive, clever recipes and ideas to get dinner on the table quickly without sacrificing flavor. Rosen's cheerful voice feels like she is beside you in the kitchen rooting you on, and that you too will get a delicious meal on the table swiftly, relying on a well-stocked pantry, smart shopping, and the occasional shortcut. Please sign me up for the Mussel and Tomato Rice Cake Toast, the Lamb and Smashed Cucumber Stuffed Pitas, and so much more."

—Colu Henry, author of *Back Pocket Pasta* and *Colu Cooks: Easy Fancy Food.*

"As a professional chef, I have always been dedicated to creating dishes from scratch without taking shortcuts. However, as a working mother of two young boys, I fully comprehend the constant struggle of ensuring our kids eat well while not sacrificing precious time. That's why *15 Minute Meals* is an absolute game-changer for parents who strive to nourish their kids without compromising on taste or quality. Packed with a treasure trove of quick and easy recipes, this book empowers you to create delectable dishes that your little ones will love. From vibrant salads to comforting soups, from flavorful pasta and noodles to an array of meat and seafood dishes all you need is 15 minutes to transform ordinary ingredients into extraordinary flavors."

—Leah Cohen, chef, tv host, and cookbook author

PRAISE FOR ROSEN'S OTHER WORKS

"Ali Rosen is saving our dinner parties one dish at a time."

—Carla Hall, chef and television host

"It's a necessary and delicious addition to any collection!"

—Kwame Onwuachi, James Beard Award—winning chef, *Top Chef* judge, and executive producer of *Food & Wine* magazine

"Ali's got us and I'm so glad that she does."

—Dorie Greenspan, author of *Baking with Dorie* and *Everyday Dorie*

"I want to give Ali Rosen a big high five for writing this book."

—Pati Jinich, James Beard Award—winning and Emmy-nominated host of *Pati's Mexican Table*

15 Minute Meals

LIST OF BOOKS BY ALI ROSEN

COOKBOOKS

Modern Freezer Meals

Bring It!

15 Minute Meals

NOVELS

Recipe for Second Chances

Alternate Endings

15 Minute Meals

Truly *Quick* Recipes that Don't Taste like Shortcuts

Ali Rosen

PUBLISHING GROUP

CORAL GABLES

Cover Design: Elina Diaz
Cover & Interior Photos: Noah Fecks
Icons: stock.adobe.com/nadiinko, stock.adobe.com/ylivdesign, stock.adobe.com/evagattuso
Layout & Design: Elina Diaz

For permission requests, please contact the publisher at:
Mango Publishing Group
2850 S Douglas Road, 2nd Floor
Coral Gables, FL 33134 USA
info@mango.bz

For special orders, quantity sales, course adoptions and corporate sales, please email the publisher at sales@mango.bz. For trade and wholesale sales, please contact Ingram Publisher Services at customer.service@ingramcontent.com or +1.800.509.4887.

15 Minute Meals: Truly Quick Recipes That Don't Taste Like Shortcuts

Library of Congress Cataloging-in-Publication number: 2023941619
ISBN: (hardcover) 978-1-68481-257-8, (paperback) 978-1-68481-338-4 (ebook) 978-1-68481-258-5
BISAC category code CKB070000, COOKING / Methods / Quick & Easy

Printed in the United States of America

To Guy, Joy, and Rae

Thank you for the privilege of getting to be your mom.

TABLE OF CONTENTS

01

HOW TO STICK
TO 15 MINUTES

Let me just get this out of the way: I love caramelized onions. My sister-in-law once joked that I should write a cookbook called, *First Start by Sautéing Some Onions*. So I am not delusional when it comes to the flavors that can develop from cooking something a long time. Slow roasted meats, simmering stocks, and, yes, deeply caramelized onions are all very dear to me.

But some days just do not have enough time for that—and that is A-okay. Quick meals do not mean you have to inevitably compromise on flavor; they just mean you can't get *some* flavors. And since we don't need every flavor every day, there's no downside to having many of your meals take only fifteen minutes. Yes, caramelized onions are delightful, but does it beat fresh summer corn cooked for two minutes on a grill? Of course not. It's different. But there's no shame in handling different ingredients differently.

Because the truth of the matter is that sometimes a fifteen-minute recipe is the only thing stopping us from eating ice cream for dinner again. Or serving a hodgepodge of leftovers and stray items on a plate as dinner. The thought of spending thirty minutes to get a cohesive meal on the table can feel daunting. Thirty minutes can be a long time. Ten minutes of prep, but then thirty minutes in the oven can feel like an impossible hurdle to overcome. And there has to be an alternative that doesn't come from a package.

So, instead of another dinner for my kids of grapes, carrot sticks, and salami (yes, I've done that), I've started trying to find where I can trim away the fat of time. What ingredients can add enough flavor to compensate for speedier cooking? What produce chars quickly? What state can my proteins be in so that they are ready without a long cook time? And once you get into that mindset, the possibilities are endless.

The mainstays I relied on have changed. No-prep vegetables like asparagus and snow peas have overshadowed others. Ground meats and thinner cuts of fish have become the default proteins. High-impact ingredients that used to require special sourcing are now readily available to add flavor when time is short. And shortcut products like minute rice, frozen vegetables, and canned ingredients have skyrocketed in quality, making them essentials in our arsenals.

Quick recipes can thrive without tasting like a compromise. You just have to know where you can get flavor quickly. And *15 Minute Meals* will be your guide.

THE KEY PREMISES

When I told people I was writing a book called *15 Minute Meals*, the skepticism was always the leader. *You mean fifteen minutes of prep time, but that doesn't include time in the oven? Or, It'll be fifteen minutes if I'm an amazing quick cook? Or, It'll take fifteen minutes once I'm done chopping everything?* And the answer to all of those is, absolutely not.

I truly, absolutely, completely know that each and every recipe in this book can be completed—start to finish, including any and all prep, with readily available ingredients—in fifteen minutes.

That doesn't mean there aren't any shortcuts (because, come on, we all need shortcuts!). That doesn't mean that, if you're a super tentative cook, it might not take you a little longer the first time around. I can't control the heat of your broiler or the speed of your stove. But I promise that this book gives you a ton of recipes you can make in fifteen minutes without any planning whatsoever, other than having the ingredients.

I do, however, have a few pieces of advice that might aid you in getting used to completing your meals within fifteen minutes.

REDUCE THE PRESSURE

Fifteen minutes is simply a guide. All of these recipes are possible (and easy) in fifteen minutes or less without being particularly speedy. But that doesn't mean you can't take your time the first time you try one. If you're a slow chopper or not a natural cook, let yourself make a recipe for the first time under less time constraint. I absolutely promise that each of these recipes will take you less than fifteen minutes once you get to know them.

YOU *NEED* A SHARP KNIFE

This shouldn't be specific to this book, and yet it seems to be the cooking item that is most commonly overlooked. Knives need to be sharpened. You don't have to be like a chef and sharpen daily (or even hourly), but you do need to sharpen with some consistency. Get an electric knife sharpener if you don't want to hone them yourself (no shame in that! They're great tools!)—I promise keeping your knives sharp will not be as large a burden as you are thinking it is.

Most importantly, you need to remember that a sharp knife is a safer knife. You can cut with more accuracy and speed if your knife is not dull. A sharp knife slips less often. Keep your knives sharp, and you'll shave off significant time from all your cooking.

GET IN THE HABIT OF USING THE WHOLE FIFTEEN MINUTES

Very few recipes in this book are set it-and-forget-it type recipes. We use the whole time. You'll notice that the ingredients list is not set up the way a normal recipe is, where prep is assumed (you'll see no ingredient called "1 chopped onion" here!). The prep is included in the recipe—you might start cooking something and then chop other ingredients as you go along. If this difference from more common recipes feels overwhelming to you, make sure to read the recipe carefully before you get started. It's meant to make it easier, but slow down when you need to.

ALL THESE MEALS ARE *MEALS*, AND THEY ARE FOR FOUR PEOPLE

There is no "serves four" in here because *every* recipe is aiming to serve four as a whole meal. But you can size up and size down—there's no baking, so you can easily half or double any recipe. Also keep in mind that portion sizes are super individual—my husband and brother typically need two full servings; my mother doesn't always finish one. Keep the people you are cooking for in mind, and the contents of the recipe. Something like rice cake toast probably won't be as filling as a chili. And these salads aren't meant to be just a side. But four people should be a good general rule of thumb.

BROILERS ARE YOUR FRIEND

Do you know why everyone loves a grill? Because it is fast, and char instantly gives flavor. Do you know what is not great about a grill? Setting it up and cleaning it up. The broiler is like a magical reverse grill. Whether you have a flame or electric oven, that high-heat blast will help you char and sizzle without ever having to go outside.

I know some ovens don't have great broilers and, if yours doesn't, then at the very least try to invest in a toaster oven—some of them now are very inexpensive and have *great* broiler functions. I promise it's worth having.

YOU CAN DO IT!

I hear so often from people that they don't know how to cook or aren't good cooks. But anyone can cook. Maybe everyone can't be (or genuinely doesn't want to be) a gourmet chef, an exquisite baker, or someone who cures their own meat. But you certainly can cook. And I'm so glad you're going to try and make your life a little more effortlessly delicious by using this book.

POWERHOUSE INGREDIENTS

While so many wonderful ingredients take quite a lot of coaxing, we are now surrounded every day by powerhouse ingredients that can make our lives easier and filled with variety.

Our access to ingredients has changed dramatically in recent decades. I love going into grocery stores whenever I travel across the country, and one of the most amazing developments in recent years is the accessibility of ingredients that once would have required a more specialty grocery store. When I was growing up, I couldn't find miso paste or harissa or tahini on my grocery store shelves. Now almost everyone can—and if you can't locally, then all of those shelf-stable ingredients are an easy two-day ship away (and possibly cheaper) from a store online.

A similar renaissance is happening even with ingredients we always had, especially canned, tinned, and frozen ingredients. You've always been able to get beans or fish in a can, but they weren't always of high quality. Now, if you make a chickpea and tuna fish salad, both star ingredients can come from cans, but those canned products can both be organic or sustainable. This revolution is similar when it comes to frozen vegetables. What once felt like a last resort is now sometimes the freshest and healthiest option available, thanks to more advanced freezing technology and higher-quality brands entering the market.

So it's a good moment to reevaluate what ingredients we use as staples—we really live in a golden era of ingredient options!

PANTRY INGREDIENTS THAT PACK A PUNCH

Often we're looking for new ways to get certain types of flavors, so below are some of my favorite ingredients that can give us a punch when we want something different. If you're unfamiliar with some of them, don't be afraid give them a try—I promise each of these is its own secret weapon in your arsenal.

UMAMI

Umami is that ineffable earthy and savory fifth taste. Umami flavors give depth and a certain craveability to a dish. These ingredients all pack that extra punch—while some of them (like anchovies, marmite, fish sauce, or MSG) can be polarizing in excess, even a little bit in a recipe can bring much-needed dimension to round everything out.

- Soy sauce
- Anchovies and anchovy paste
- Tomato paste
- Miso
- Olives
- Fish sauce
- Seaweed
- MSG
- Garlic powder
- Marmite
- Cured meats like prosciutto and salami

UNCTUOUSNESS

Some dishes need a bit of richness to make them sing. These unctuous ingredients add smooth and soft texture and flavor.

- Tahini
- Olive oil
- Molasses
- Butter
- Lard
- Schmaltz (or chicken fat)

SPICY

Bring on the heat! Whether it's fire or tingle or a hint of pepper, there's more flavor in spiciness than we often give credence to.

- Gojuchang
- Sriracha
- Harissa
- Chili crisp
- Hot sauce

ACIDITY

Those puckery, sharp flavors that brighten up a dish often make it fly. They can add freshness and balance bitterness and sweetness. Acidic ingredients elevate heavier recipes and form a cornerstone of necessity in any dish.

- Citrus, like lemons and limes
- Ginger paste
- Tamarind paste
- Hoisin sauce
- Pomegranate molasses
- Vinegars of all kinds—cider, balsamic, rice, red wine, etc.
- Sour cream
- Pickles

DON'T DISCOUNT THE JAR

Canned and jarred foods have a reputation as being lower quality, but the key is to know what you're looking for. Yes, there are some packaged products with a lot of additives and lesser ingredients. But in recent years there has been a boom of products that focus on sustainability, careful sourcing, and leaving out the sodium and unnecessary preservatives. If you know what you're looking for, you can get a central part of your meal in a can without compromising on quality.

CANNED BEANS

Look for organic versions with low sodium. There should only be three ingredients in canned beans—the bean itself, water, and salt.

TINNED SEAFOOD

Tuna and anchovies have been a popular staple for a long time, but take it from the Spanish and Portuguese and enjoy this classic preservation for a wider array of seafood, from clams to mussels to fish. Look for a sustainable label (easily delineated with the MSC blue fish or the Friend of the Sea sailboat logos, which both have good standards) and fish that are packed in oil.

JARRED VEGETABLES

While I prefer frozen for many of the more delicate vegetables (give me a frozen green bean or corn over canned any day), jarring vegetables has been an essential historic technique that's just gotten a bad rap. And in recent years we've seen higher-quality versions of some of the best items to jar—whole tomatoes, sundried tomatoes, peppers, artichokes, hearts of palm, okra, onions, and beets. Sometimes jarred products, when prepared properly, bring their own unique flavor that stands out from the raw version. Just make sure to look for few to no additives.

FROZEN CAN BE BETTER

I might be biased, having written an entire other cookbook about frozen food, but I think frozen food is another major area where we need to retool our thinking.

FROZEN VEGETABLES

When vegetables are frozen, they are frozen at the peak of their freshness. That sometimes means you're getting a better version frozen than you'd get from the fresh produce section, both in flavor and often in nutritional content. The key is knowing which vegetables work best from frozen. Low-moisture vegetables like peas, beans, corn, and broccoli tend to hold up best in this context.

FROZEN SEAFOOD

Like vegetables, seafood gets frozen at its peak. So that can often mean your fish out of the freezer is much better preserved than the fish sitting at your grocery store counter that has been out of the water for almost a week (or even, more often than you'd think, frozen and defrosted to then sit at your grocery fish counter).

ALLOW YOURSELF THE EASY HEFT

A lot of people feel like they need that classic plate of protein, vegetable, and starch. And while I can't argue with that balance, I can certainly advocate for making the heft (usually the starch) a bit easier.

BREAD

You *do not have to cook* to have a starch on the side of your meal. Bread is a totally acceptable starch, and sometimes nothing is better than making a quick meal and sopping up the sauce with bread. Don't think you have to do more than that.

PASTA AND NOODLES

I don't think I have to convince anyone of the joys and ease of pasta, but keep in mind that some versions cook easier than others. Thin dried wheat, egg, rice noodles, ramen, and vermicelli all cook in mere minutes. And fresh pasta is not only more readily available, but much quicker. The good news on all of these fronts is that the quality of quick products is improving constantly—look for buzzwords that indicate quality, like lack of additives and preservatives, organic ingredients, or air-dried noodles.

MINUTE OR FROZEN RICE

I won't argue that there aren't differences in taste and texture depending on how you cook your rice. But the minute or frozen versions are so convenient and still pretty delicious. Don't get hung up on a recipe just because you don't want to take twenty minutes making the rice—the easy subs do just fine.

COUSCOUS, FONIO, BULGUR, AND OTHER GRAINS

There are so many quick-cooking grains. Some, like fonio, barely even take five minutes! If you're stuck in a rice or noodle rut (not that there's anything wrong with that), find some variety in a slew of grains that are now much more readily available.

POLENTA ROLLS

This is like the bread of the grain world—you truly don't have to do *anything*. You could eat it straight from the package. If you want some heft—especially a non-glutinous option—look out for polenta rolls. They're one of the easiest additions to a meal.

HEFT DOESN'T HAVE TO BE A STARCH

Nuts, cucumbers, beans, and more can add a whole lot of easy heft too. If you need a dish to be filling, throw in one of these innocuous ingredients and it'll fit almost every time.

INVEST IN BETTER INGREDIENTS

This is almost as important as the rest, even though I know this isn't always possible and a budget is a budget.

But hear me out: when we are talking about simplifying our cooking, often what that means is that the base state of our ingredients becomes that much more important. Think of the quality of salmon you might use for sushi versus a salmon burger. 15 minute meals are the same—if you're making simple tacos, go for the organic or smaller batch taco shells; if you're making cacio e pepe, get the real parmesan and buy the local tomatoes instead of the cheaper variety that have been sitting all week.

It doesn't mean every ingredient needs to be expensive (hello, didn't I just mention frozen vegetables over fresh?), but it does mean that you should look at ingredient lists and allow simple ingredients to sing.

A NOTE ON SPICES

We all rely on spices for flavor, and that hardly needs to be reiterated, but there is one important thing that often gets forgotten: spices have a shelf life and come in different qualities. No, that paprika you bought three years ago from the grocery store brand is probably not going to give you as much flavor as the new, thoughtfully sourced one.

Luckily, the options for great spices now are expanding, and we are truly lucky to have access that we never did before. Companies like Burlap and Barrel, Spice House, and DiasporaCo are really completely upending our expectations and are just an online click away. So if there's one area where you might want to up your game a bit, I'd start with spices.

IT'S OKAY THAT SOME INGREDIENTS CAN'T BE FAST

Look, no number of shortcuts is ever going to get you a quick pulled pork. My aforementioned beloved caramelized onions cannot be hacked. And a lot of the shortcuts we wish were good—I'm looking at you, pre-minced garlic and fake lemon juice—just will never make the grade.

That's really okay. There are times when you want to bake your own bread or make a multi-day sauce. Not everything can find a faster way to us. So if you're hung up on a highly particular thing, then please just spend the time. Because, I promise, there are so many other delicious things out there that will be quick for you when you're ready to focus your attention elsewhere.

SHORTCUTS ARE OKAY

Let's breathe in and imagine a world where some things have been made easier for us. Doesn't that sound great? Of course it does. So why wouldn't we accept that help?

If there is anything in this book that can make your life easier, I am all for it. If you want to buy something pre-chopped, pre-made, pre-cooked, *whatever*, I say go for it. If fifteen minutes feels too long and you have some piece of a meal that can make it shorter for you, then there is no judgment.

FIND YOUR OWN LITTLE WAYS TO SAVE TIME

Do you have a slow stovetop? Put water on to boil before you take off your shoes. Disorganized? Pull out all your ingredients before you get started cooking. Spending all your time at the grocery store, no matter how quick the recipes are? Look into a grocery delivery service or save money by swapping shop times with a friend or neighbor.

And I'm going to throw this one out there even though I know some people (ahem, my sister) are going to gag. If you are buying nicer produce (hello, farmers markets!), a little bit of dirt won't hurt you. I rinse my herbs and produce a lot less when I know they're good-quality, and that actually is one of my biggest time-savers.

FUDGE THE NUMBERS

Have a fourteen-ounce can instead of a fifteen-ounce one? That's fine! Want to eyeball the amount of ricotta in a pasta instead of making another measuring cup dirty? You're the boss! None of these recipes are exact science. We're not baking a layer cake that needs to stand up (literally). Everything is to your taste, so don't waste time where you don't need to.

INVEST IN TIME-SAVING KITCHEN EQUIPMENT

We often think of prep and cooking time as the thing that eats away at our day. But we often don't realize the places where we can invest once and save a lot of time in the long run.

TOASTER OVEN

If your broiler takes too long to heat up, get a toaster oven—they often have some of the fastest and best broiler settings to go along with your toast.

A HIGH-QUALITY BLENDER

The quality of a blender can make a huge difference. The sharpness of the blades, the power of the motor, and the temperature control can all speed up recipes. I throw whole produce into my blender and that has saved me a ton of time. So if you're looking for a place to splurge, a good blender really can add value.

GRIDDLE PAN

A lot of recipes require a lot of surface area. Using two pans adds pain to cleanup, and juggling multiple servings can just add time. So get a griddle pan to go across two burners, and do twice as much on one surface.

KNIFE SHARPENER

I know I mentioned this earlier, but it bears repeating: a sharp knife is safer and significantly faster. Sharpen your knives every few weeks at home, and the time will add up.

HOW TO USE THIS BOOK

The goal of this book is to make your life easier and more delicious. Every recipe here takes fifteen minutes or less—that's a given.

But of course, we can't account for the time it takes to choose a recipe, shop for ingredients, and clean up. Yet, I'm still going to try and make even those things easier for you. Every recipe includes a few badges that will give an indication of some of its superpowers as well as a showcase of what kitchen items you need that will require extra washing up.

THE RECIPE BADGES

ONE PAN

Everyone's favorite kind of recipe. If you see this badge, you know you've only got to worry about cleaning up a single pan for whatever you're cooking.

NO CHOPPING

Some days, you really want to throw everything together and not take out the dang knife. So if you see this badge, you'll know your cutting board can stay in the drawer.

NO COOK

Sometimes we just can't be bothered to turn on the oven or the stove. Who needs heat when you can have no cooking involved at all? If you see this badge, you know you'll be throwing everything together without turning anything on.

PANTRY HERO

These are recipes where almost all the ingredients come from the pantry or are items you'd have on hand. So look out for this symbol if you're scrounging on an evening when your fresh groceries might be low, or if you want to plan ahead to always have certain items in your cupboard.

FIT FOR GUESTS

 These are recipes that present a little nicer, that don't *look* like a 15 minute meal. Sometimes we really need a quick meal that also looks like we tried a little harder, so, if you see this badge, you'll know you're in the clear.

MIX AND MATCH

 These are recipes whose flavors can be mixed and matched into different combos. The starch portion of these recipes could be a taco, rice bowl, toast, or the carb-free lettuce wrap. Take the ingredients for the toast and throw them in a lettuce wrap. Grab the ingredients from the tacos and top a rice bowl with them instead.

FREEZER FRIENDLY

 Since getting ingredients is half the battle, sometimes we want to make a 15 minute meal and eat some now and save some for later. So if you see this badge, you'll know you can freeze the recipe too.

THE KITCHEN ITEM BADGES

Look out for these icons to show you what you'll have to use (a.k.a. wash!) in every recipe.

We have icons for:

 KNIFE   **BROILER/SHEET PAN**

 BOWLS   **MIXER**

 POTS AND PANS   **MICROWAVE**

 BLENDER   **GRATER**

02
SALADS

02

SALADS

BROILED ROMAINE *with* GORGONZOLA *and* PISTACHIOS

Broiling romaine unlocks a world of meal possibilities—it is crunchy, hearty, and healthy, and takes on a char within minutes. It is a textured canvas for flavor. I love draping it in the combination of tangy pomegranate molasses, nutty pistachios, and creamy gorgonzola dolce. It all combines for a perfectly balanced bite with essentially no work. If you can't find pomegranate molasses (although you should definitely track it down, since it is one of the most versatile ingredients), you can sub in balsamic vinegar for a similar note of acidic sweetness. Also try to seek out gorgonzola dolce, or another creamy blue cheese, so you can get that melty goodness.

Ingredients

3 heads of romaine

Drizzle of extra-virgin olive oil

Heavy drizzle pomegranate molasses

Dash of Kosher salt

1 cup (140 g/5 oz) shelled pistachios

½ pound (225 g/8 oz) gorgonzola dolce

Make sure the top rack of your oven is as high as it can go. Turn on your broiler. Slice your romaine heads in half (if they are especially large you can do thirds or quarters). Place aluminum foil on a sheet pan. Add the romaine on top (cut side up) and drizzle with olive oil, pomegranate molasses, and a generous sprinkle of salt. Put the romaine under the broiler and cook for two to three minutes, or until the lettuce has started to char.

While the lettuce is cooking, roughly chop the pistachios. Remove the romaine from the oven and crumble the gorgonzola on top. Add another drizzle of pomegranate molasses and finish with the pistachios on top. Put under the broiler for one more minute. Remove and serve hot.

CUCUMBER *and*
CHICKPEA SEAFOOD SALAD

Somewhere along the way, canned seafood turned into tinned seafood and became trendy again. But it's always been a delicious, fast, and economical way to enjoy seafood. It's just now more widely available at a higher quality. So look for something wild and preferably sustainable (I like the MSC little blue fish label from the Marine Stewardship Council), and you'll have a filling salad meal. Make sure you have a sharp knife, since this recipe involves a lot of smashing and dicing (and maybe is not for the slow choppers among us).

Ingredients

1 small red onion

1 cup (250 mL/8 oz) cider vinegar

Dash of Kosher salt

10 Persian cucumbers (or 2 English cucumbers)

2 15-oz (400 g) cans chickpeas

8 oz (200 g) tinned mussels

2 5-oz (145 g) cans tuna (packed in oil preferably)

Heavy drizzle extra-virgin olive oil

Small bunch chives

Small bunch parsley

Chop the red onion. Place the red onion in a bowl with the cider vinegar and a dash of salt. Make sure the onion pieces are fully submerged (you can add more cider vinegar as needed). Let them sit for at least five minutes.

Using the side of a knife (or bottom of a frying pan), smash the cucumbers and then roughly chop them so they are bite-size. Drain the chickpeas, mussels, and tuna and then add them to a bowl with the olive oil. Chop the chives and parsley and add them in. Add a generous dash of salt. Add the onions, along with 3 tablespoons of the vinegar liquid, into the salad and combine. Taste to see if you need more salt or vinegar.

DICED FENNEL *and* POMEGRANATE SALAD

I like to think of this as the negroni of salads. It's got that addictive bitterness matched with eye-popping color. Serve it on its own, or throw in some chicken or a side of bread to pump it up. But I love the simplicity of having this as a meal—by finely chopping the fennel, and with the tartness of pomegranate seeds throughout, you get tons of flavor melding into every bite. Take the shortcut here and buy the pomegranate seeds. You'll be left with a meal as uncomplicated as whipping out your cutting board.

Ingredients

2 anchovy fillets (preferably from an oil-packed pack of anchovies)

2 tablespoons Greek yogurt

1 lemon

1 tablespoon balsamic vinegar

¼ cup (60 mL/2 oz) extra-virgin olive oil

1 small head of radicchio

1 fennel bulb

½ cup (80 g/3 oz) pomegranate seeds

½ cup (80 g/3 oz) walnuts

Dash of Kosher salt

In a shakable container, add the anchovy fillets and the Greek yogurt. Smush the anchovies into the yogurt with a fork or whisk (if you want them to really meld in, you can always throw the whole dressing in the blender). Juice the lemon in and add the balsamic vinegar and olive oil. Shake thoroughly to combine.

Lightly chop the radicchio and place in a bowl. Chop the fennel bulb more finely (the smaller the pieces, the better). Add the fennel, pomegranate seeds, and walnuts to the bowl with the radicchio. Toss the dressing in with a dash of salt and combine fully.

BLACK-EYED PEA SALAD

Where I grew up, in South Carolina's Lowcountry, there's a New Year's Day tradition that involves boiling black-eyed peas with collard greens and rice into a stewy dish called Hoppin' John. It's supposed to bring good luck. I've always loved the combination, and I don't get why we don't bring those flavors into other times of year. This salad is inspired by that tradition, but in a brighter form. We use canned peas, fresh cherry tomatoes, and a pork hit from Canadian bacon to get a dish that speeds up and lightens up a winter classic. It's not traditional, but it's quick, filling, and perfect for bringing all of those time-honored flavors into a new light.

Ingredients

12 oz (340 g) cauliflower rice

Dash of olive oil

Dash of Kosher salt

1 bunch collards

4 tablespoons apple cider vinegar

1 large lemon

1 ½ cups cherry tomatoes (350 g/ 12 oz)

6 oz Canadian bacon
(around six thick slices)

2 15-oz (400 g) cans of black-eyed peas

Place a wide saucepan on medium high heat and add the cauliflower rice, along with olive oil and a heavy dash of salt. Cook for three minutes, or until the cauliflower rice has softened but still has a bite to it. When it's done, set it to the side to cool.

While the rice is cooking, chop the collards—you want them to be heavily chopped. Put them in a large bowl with another dash of salt, the cider vinegar, and the juice of the lemon. Halve the cherry tomatoes and slice the Canadian bacon into bite-sized pieces. Add both to the bowl. Drain the cans of black-eyed peas and then add them into the bowl along with the cauliflower rice (if the rice is still a bit warm, it's okay). Stir to combine, and taste to see if any additional salt or vinegar is needed.

TABBOULEH SALAD *with* APPLE, WALNUTS, *and* CILANTRO

Let's just say right off the bat that this is not in any traditional way a tabbouleh—but since that's the name we know, I'm hoping it gives everyone an entry point into the world of bulgur wheat in salads. The nutty textured grain adds heft and flavor to a dish that balances earthy walnuts with the sweetness of apples. If you don't like cilantro, you can certainly replace it with other herbs—this does well with mint (although maybe half the amount) or basil. Either way, it's a vegetarian quick dream that works well warm or saved for later and pulled from the fridge

Ingredients

1 ½ cups (275 g/ 10 oz) bulgur wheat (medium or fine grain)

Dash of Kosher salt

2 large apples (honeycrisp preferred)

Large bunch of cilantro

1 cup (160 g/6 oz) walnut pieces

1 large lemon

4 cups (80 g/ 3 oz) arugula

Heavy drizzle extra-virgin olive oil

Put 3 cups (700 mL/24 oz) of water and the bulgur wheat in a large pot with a heavy dash of salt. Bring the water up to a boil. Cover the pot and then reduce the heat to medium, so everything simmers. It should take about ten minutes to cook.

While the bulgur is cooking, dice the apples and lightly cut the cilantro. Chop the walnut pieces if yours are on the larger side.

When the bulgur is about a minute from being done (most of the water should be absorbed), juice the lemon on top. Cover again for a minute and then remove the pot from the heat. Add the apples, cilantro, walnuts, arugula, and olive oil. Stir together and taste to see if more salt is needed. Serve warm or refrigerate for later.

AVOCADO CRAB SALAD

I think of lump crab meat as a great hidden secret for dinnertime—it's one of the few proteins you can buy ready to go and add heft and flavor into any dish. I love this salad because it delights in an abundance of texture without a lot of work—the apples and romaine naturally have a crispness, while the potato chips give a salty crunch. It's surprising and bursting with flavor at every turn. And it goes well with a side of bread if you need something more filling with your meal.

Ingredients

2 heads of romaine lettuce

2 large apples (honeycrisp or other crunchy variety preferred)

3 avocados

2 cups (500 g/ 16 oz) lump crab meat

2 teaspoons cumin

⅓ cup (80 mL/ 2.7 oz) sherry vinegar

Heavy dash of Kosher salt

Heavy drizzle of olive oil

1 cup (34 g/ 1.2 oz) potato chips

Dice the ingredients that need to be diced—the romaine, apples, and avocado. Put the romaine and apples into a bowl and add the crab meat, cumin, sherry vinegar, dash of salt, and drizzle of olive oil. Combine gently. Add the avocado and gently fold it in. Taste to see if any additional salt is needed. Lightly crumble the potato chips on top and serve immediately.

SMOKED SALMON, FETA, *and* CUCUMBER SALAD

I like to think of this as the healthy quick alternative to an everything bagel with lox. This salad hits the same salty and savory notes, but with a slightly healthier bent. Feta replaces cream cheese here to give a briny kick that will have you (almost) not notice you're without a bagel. If you have everything bagel seasoning already, you can sub that in here and spend even less time making this recipe (1 to 2 tablespoons should do it). And if you want a bit more substance, you can always throw in some croutons or crushed pita chips to add some heft.

Ingredients

2 lemons

½ teaspoon garlic powder

2 teaspoons poppy seeds

½ teaspoon onion powder

2 teaspoons sesame seeds

½ teaspoon Kosher salt

⅓ cup (80 mL / 2.7 oz) extra-virgin olive oil

10 Persian cucumbers
(or 2 English cucumbers)

8 oz (250 g) smoked salmon

Bibb or Boston lettuce

5 oz (140 g) crumbled feta

2 tablespoons capers

Into a bowl, juice the lemons. Then add the garlic powder, poppy seeds, onion powder, sesame seeds, salt, and olive oil, and whisk until combined. Slice the cucumbers and cut the smoked salmon into small pieces. Combine with the lettuce, feta, capers, and dressing.

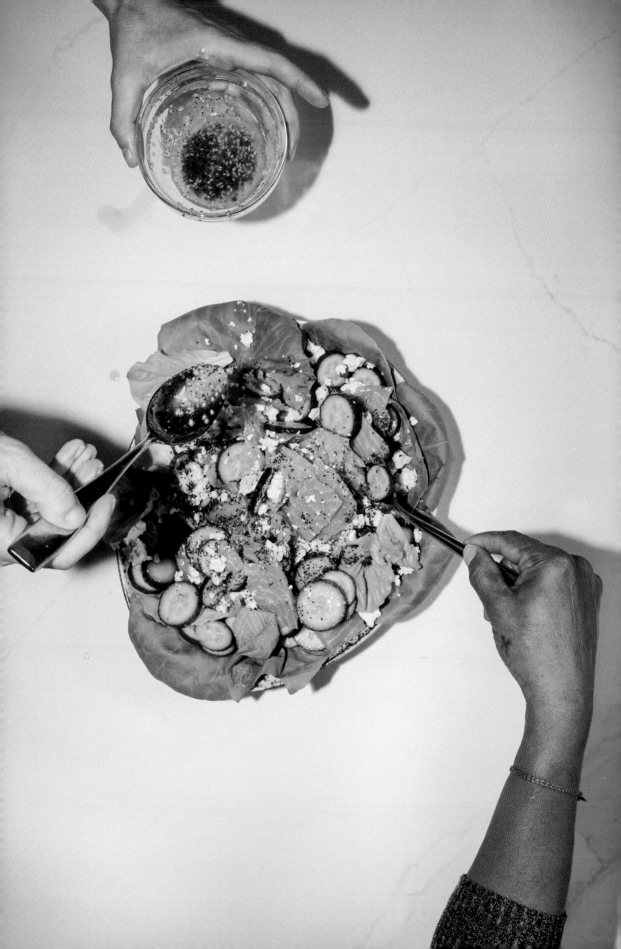

CHARRED CABBAGE *with* WHIPPED FETA

One of my favorite restaurants, Butcher and Bee, has this whipped feta appetizer that is addictive. The tangy brine of feta melds sensationally with the sweet heat of hot honey. I've always thought a similar combination could top a particularly robust salad, and with cabbage and the crunch of pecans, it really does the trick. It's a dish that is surprising, filled with flavor, and addictive—all elements that are often hard to find in a fifteen-minute salad.

Ingredients

1 large head of green cabbage

Dash of olive oil, plus additional

Dash of Kosher salt

4 oz (110 g) feta

4 oz (110 g) cream cheese

2 tablespoons mint

2 tablespoons honey

1 teaspoon hot sauce (plus additional as you prefer)

1 cup (140 g/5 oz) pecans

Turn on your oven's broiler, making sure your top rack is close to the flame. Chop the cabbage roughly into bite-sized pieces. Line a sheet pan with aluminum foil and toss the cabbage on top with a pour of olive oil and a heavy sprinkle of salt. Place the cabbage under the broiler for four to ten minutes, depending on the heat of your broiler and how close you want to put it (I like getting close, but I know it makes others wary!). It should be charred and cooked, but still with a bit of crunch when it is done.

While the cabbage is cooking, make the sauce. Using a mixer (or by hand with a fork if you don't mind stirring a lot!), combine the feta and cream cheese in a bowl until it is whipped and a bit fluffy. You can add a few tablespoons of olive oil if it doesn't have the lightness you would like. Chop the mint and add that to the mixture as well. In a separate small bowl, combine the honey and hot sauce. Finally, crush or chop the pecans roughly.

When the cabbage is done, remove it from the oven and, while it is still hot, put it into a bowl. Combine with the feta mixture and the pecans—the cabbage should melt the feta a bit so that it is all easy to combine evenly.

Serve either as one large bowl or split into individual bowls, but finish by drizzling the hot honey on top.

ANCHOVY STUFFED PEPPERS
with GREENS

Sometimes the antipasto in Italy is the best part of the meal, so I wanted to twist a classic idea into a salad that can double as a light meal. Roasted red peppers are always brimming with flavor, and the broiler does the trick here. With a tomato, anchovy, and garlic center inside, you'll have so much packed into one package. It's really that simple, over a bed of baby kale with a drizzle of lemon and olive oil to round it out.

Ingredients

4 bell peppers

Dash of extra-virgin olive oil

Dash of Kosher salt

¾ cup (175 g/ 6 oz) cherry tomatoes

2 oz anchovies (preferably
the kind packed in oil)

2 cloves garlic

Large bunch basil

½ (30 g) cup panko bread crumbs

½ cup (50 g) grated parmesan cheese

6 cups (120 g/ 4 oz) baby kale

1 lemon

Turn on your oven's broiler. Line a sheet tray with aluminum foil.

Cut the tops off the bell peppers and slice them in half. Remove the seeds, but don't feel the need to trim the peppers (they cook enough that it doesn't really matter). Place the peppers on the sheet tray, skin side up, and drizzle with a bit of olive oil and a dash of salt. Place in the oven for two minutes.

While the peppers are cooking, in a blender, combine the tomatoes, anchovies, garlic, and basil (you can leave the basil stems on, so don't worry about cutting them).

Remove the peppers from the oven, turn them over, and spoon in the tomato-anchovy mixture. Top with the bread crumbs and then parmesan cheese. Drizzle another helping of olive oil on top with another dash of salt. Place the sheet tray back in the oven for another three minutes or until the bread crumbs have begun to brown.

While the peppers are cooking, toss the kale with the juice of the lemon, another dash of olive oil, and a bit of salt. When done, remove the peppers and plate them on top of the kale.

SPICY COLLARDS CAESAR SALAD

This is a quick and hearty twist on a beloved recipe. Take the creamy perfection of Caesar dressing and hike up the spice a bit with a jalapeño. Collards are an inexpensive and healthy alternative that bulk up the proceedings (and trust me, if you love kale—which you could also use here—you're missing out if you're skipping collards). The crunch of celery and the toasted panko bread crumbs take it all up a notch so you get that crunchy, spicy, creamy combo that can't be beat. Add on any proteins like grilled chicken or salmon if you want something even more.

Ingredients

2 tablespoons unsalted butter

1 cup (60 g) panko bread crumbs

Dash of Kosher salt

⅓ cup (33 g) parmesan

½ cup (104 g/3.6 oz) mayonnaise

1 lemon

4 anchovy fillets (try to get the ones packed in oil)

1 small jalapeño or serrano pepper (or more or less to your taste)

1 bunch of collards

2 stalks of celery

Place a small saucepan on medium high heat and add the butter. When the butter has melted, add the bread crumbs and a dash of salt. Toast the bread crumbs, stirring occasionally, for approximately five minutes, or until the bread crumbs are lightly golden brown.

While the bread crumbs are cooking, in a blender, combine the parmesan, mayonnaise, juice of the lemon, anchovy, and the pepper (or more or less pepper, depending on your tolerance for heat). Chop the collards—you want to use a sharp knife and cut them roughly into bite-sized small pieces. Then chop the celery, also into small pieces. Combine the dressing with the collards and the celery. Top with the bread crumbs and serve.

The KING *and* I SALAD

I'm from Charleston, SC, and every time I go home I have to go to Leon's, a restaurant renowned for its fried chicken and oysters. But while I love those main events, somehow I and everyone in my family always ends up ordering this particular salad, called the Siam Salad. If you tell people you're obsessed with a cabbage, peanut, and orange salad, they might look at you like you're crazy, but there's something about the combination that just sings. The Leon's version has incredible fried shallots, which obviously could not fit into a fifteen-minute version (although you certainly can buy some great versions online or at Asian supermarkets, which would up the oomph here). So this is a faster take on it, with panko subbing in. This name is a backward ode to the original name—the salad got its name because Leon's is situated on the corner of King Street and I Street, and so it was a nod to the brilliant musical, cheekily named after where the titular King is from.

Ingredients

2 avocados

4 clementines or small seedless oranges

Bunch of mint leaves

3 limes

2 tablespoons sesame oil

2 tablespoons extra-virgin olive oil

Dash of Kosher salt

6 to 8 cups shredded cabbage
(or two 10-oz/283 g bags)

½ cup (70 g/2.5 oz) roasted salted peanuts

1 cup (60 g) panko crumbs

Cut the avocados into pieces. Peel the clementines and break them into segments. Chop the mint.

In a small bowl, juice the limes. Add the mint, sesame oil, olive oil, and a dash of salt. Stir to combine.

Add the cabbage, peanuts, panko crumbs, clementines, and lime dressing into a bowl. Stir to combine. Add the avocado last and gently stir it in.

CHILI CHICKEN *and*
BLACK BEAN SALAD

Buying thinly cut chicken is one of the great fast-meal cheats. When I have more time, I love a bone-in cut, but this salad utilizes the speed of the broiler to make chicken fast. This is one of those recipes that has a little bit of everything—a bit of crunch, a hint of spice, a jolt of freshness, and the brightness of vinegar.

Ingredients

2 pounds (900 g/32 oz) chicken tenders or thin chicken cutlets

16 oz (450 g) frozen corn

2 teaspoons chili powder

Salt to taste (but at least a teaspoon)

1 large bunch lacinato (Tuscan) kale

2 14-oz (400 g) cans black beans

1 cup (92 g/3 oz) sliced almonds

¼ cup (60 mL/2 oz) apple cider vinegar (plus additional as needed)

Drizzle of olive oil

Make sure your oven rack is as high as it can go, and turn on your oven's broiler. Line a sheet tray with foil. Spread the chicken and corn on the sheet tray (making sure all ingredients are as flat as possible). Spread the chili powder and some salt on both sides of the chicken as well as on the corn. Place under the broiler in the oven—broil for two minutes on each side (or more or less, depending on the power of your broiler. You want it to be just cooked through and not overcooked).

While the chicken and corn are in the oven, chop the kale and drain the black beans. Place the kale and beans into a bowl with the almonds, cider vinegar, olive oil, and another dash of salt.

Remove the chicken and corn from the oven. Slice the chicken into bite-sized pieces. Add the chicken and corn to the salad (it's okay if it's still a little hot). Stir and taste—add more vinegar and salt as needed.

03
SOUPS

GINGERY CHICKEN *and* RICE SOUP

This is the quick version of the comfort food classic. A good chicken stock is an essential base, but since we are trying to keep it as easy as possible, there is also ton of flavor added through the coconut milk, ginger, garlic, and fish sauce. Those powerhouse ingredients make up for any lack of length in cooking time. The secret here is to just buzz almost everything up in the blender—you don't even need to peel your ginger. Then you heat it all together and you're ready to go. I'm a fan of leftover white rice from ordering in, but this also works great with minute rice or frozen rice (although if you're making it with frozen, make sure to add an extra few minutes). Same goes for the chicken—if you have leftovers in your fridge, shred them up and throw them in instead of the ground chicken. Either way, it's the perfect break from long stewing times.

Ingredients

1 pound (454 g/ 16 oz) ground chicken

1 ½ teaspoons Kosher salt

1 14-oz (400 g) can coconut milk

2-inch knob of fresh ginger
(or about 1 tablespoon)

4 garlic cloves

1 tablespoon fish sauce

3 cups (750 mL/ 24 oz) chicken stock

2 cups (500 g/ 16 oz) cooked jasmine rice

2 large scallions

In a wok or large pot on medium high heat, add in the chicken and stir occasionally. While the chicken is cooking, put the salt, coconut milk, ginger, garlic, and fish sauce into a blender and fully combine. Mix with the chicken stock. Chop the scallions.

After five minutes, or whenever the chicken is almost fully cooked, add the rice, the scallions, and the stock mixture to the pot. Bring up to a heavy simmer. If your rice was not frozen, it should be ready to serve; if you started from frozen, you may need a few extra minutes. Serve immediately.

SPICED-UP TURKEY CHILI

The one meal almost everyone can agree on is chili. And while some like to stew for a long time, turkey does well when it is cooked quickly. So this is mostly just pouring everything into a pot and letting the flavors work on their own. If you don't have anchovy paste, you can always sub in Worcestershire or fish sauce to get that extra hit of umami—you do need it, since turkey doesn't have as much flavor as some other meats.

Ingredients

Dash of extra-virgin olive oil

2 pounds (900 g/32 oz) ground turkey

Kosher salt (at least 1 to 2 teaspoons, more as needed)

1 tablespoon garlic powder

1 tablespoon onion powder

2 teaspoons chili powder

1 tablespoon anchovy paste

1 28-oz (794 g) can diced tomatoes

2 15-oz (400 g) cans kidney beans

¼ cup (60 mL/2 oz) apple cider vinegar

To a large stockpot on medium high heat, add the olive oil, turkey, salt, garlic powder, onion powder, chili powder, and anchovy paste and cook for five to seven minutes, or until the turkey has browned a bit.

Drain the tomatoes and kidney beans, but reserve their liquid if you like a soupier chili. Add the tomatoes, kidney beans, and cider vinegar to the pot. Bring up to a low boil and cook for five more minutes, uncovered, stirring occasionally. If you want the chili to have a soupier quality, you can add back in some of the reserved bean and tomato liquid. Add more salt to taste and serve hot.

CUCUMBER YOGURT SOUP

Sometimes you want a light and refreshing soup, and the bonus to that is that you don't need to cook anything—in fact, all you need is a quick blitz in the blender! This recipe is like tzatziki in soup form, filled to the brim with zesty herbaceousness. Eat it with a side of pita and you'll have a whole meal in a soup.

Ingredients

8 Persian cucumbers (or 2 large seedless cucumbers)

1 ½ cups (350 g/ 12 oz) Greek yogurt

1 lemon

3 garlic cloves

Small bunch basil

Small bunch mint

Small bunch chives

1 teaspoon Kosher salt, plus more as needed

Drizzle of olive oil

Pita (optional)

Put the cucumbers, yogurt, the juice of the lemon, garlic, basil, mint, chives, and salt into a blender and fully blend (if you don't have the strongest blender, you may want to roughly chop the cucumbers before starting). Taste to see if additional salt or herbs are needed (I like an extra half teaspoon of salt here, but it's up to your preference).

You can serve at room temperature, or store in the fridge for up to two days and serve cold. When serving, top with a drizzle of olive oil and any additional garnishes you'd like, such as more chopped herbs or cucumbers. Serve with pita or other bread to make it a full meal.

The QUICKEST DROP DUMPLINGS

I know dumplings seem impossible in fifteen minutes, but drop dumplings really are that simple. They're like a cross between a biscuit and a traditional dumpling—not shaped, not fancy, and not time-consuming. The key to this is having a good broth—since the dumplings absorb the liquid, you need to have a proper base. From there, you can add anything else you want to this; it's perfect for leftovers like shredded chicken or stray frozen veggies. Jazz it up with herbs or spices, since this recipe is a base that can really handle flavor additions.

Ingredients

6 cups (1.5 L / 48 oz) broth (make sure it's a good-quality broth and salted well)

2 tablespoons butter

1 cup (150 g) flour

½ teaspoon Kosher salt, plus additional

½ tablespoon baking powder

½ cup (125 mL / 4 oz) whole milk

Chives and parsley for garnish

Put the broth on medium high heat. Add salt to taste, and any vegetables you may want to include. (I like a big handful of spinach, but anything works here.) Bring up to a low boil.

While the broth is heating, melt the butter in the microwave. In a separate bowl, whisk together the flour, salt, and baking powder. Add in the milk and the melted butter and mix until just combined. Spoon out the dough into small balls, about the size of a tablespoon (you don't need to shape them any more than just scooping with a spoon—drop dumplings aren't meant to be symmetrical!), and drop the dumplings by the spoonful into the broth. Cook for four to five minutes, or until the dumplings fully float.

While the dumplings are cooking, chop chives or parsley as desired. Serve immediately, tasting to see if you need any additional salt, then sprinkling any herbs on top.

PINTO BEAN, TOMATO, *and* AVOCADO SOUP

A good soup relies on being filling, flavorful, and bursting with texture, and this one has all those elements in spades, despite its quick cook. Avocado often only gets used in cold contexts, but it works wonders in a soup. Add a bit of spice and the freshness of cilantro, and you have a keeper that you'll continuously come back to on a cold day.

Ingredients

2 15-oz (400 g) cans of pinto beans

4 small to medium vine-ripened tomatoes

3 garlic cloves

1 teaspoon fennel seed

1 teaspoon cumin

1 teaspoon chili powder

2 cups (450 mL/ 16 oz) vegetable broth

Dash of Kosher salt

Large bunch cilantro

2 avocados

In a blender (or in a pot with an immersion blender), combine 1 can of pinto beans, including the liquid, 2 tomatoes, the garlic, fennel seed, cumin, chili powder, broth, and salt. Make sure it is fully blended. Transfer to a pot and turn on the heat to medium high.

While the soup is heating, chop the remaining tomatoes. Add the tomatoes and the other can of pinto beans along with its liquid into the pot. While that heats up (only to a strong simmer, never a boil), roughly chop the cilantro and then dice the avocado.

Taste the soup to make sure you don't need more salt (some bean liquid has it and some doesn't, so it can vary), and then put the soup into bowls. Add the cilantro and avocado on top and serve hot.

CHORIZO CHICKPEA STEW

Chorizo is a perfect powerhouse ingredient—it has spice, it has piquancy, and, since it's already cooked, it's the simplest sausage around. This stew is rounded out with peppers, chickpeas, and chopped tomatoes to create a meld that gives you an entire well-rounded meal in a bowl. If you want it a little less meaty, you can always up the chickpeas and reduce the chorizo, but either way you'll have a bright, beautiful bowl in a flash.

Ingredients

12 oz (340 g) chorizo

5 oz (142 g) spinach (fresh or frozen both work fine)

1 12-oz (340 g) jar of roasted red pepper

1 15-oz (400 g) can of chickpeas

1 ½ cups (375 mL/12 oz) chicken stock

1 28-oz can (794 g) chopped tomatoes

Dash of Kosher salt

Place a large skillet or wok on high heat. Slice the chorizo into bite-sized pieces and then add it to the skillet along with the spinach. Cook for three to five minutes. While the chorizo is cooking, roughly chop the red peppers and add them into the skillet. Drain the chickpeas.

When the chorizo has browned, add the chickpeas, chicken stock, and chopped tomatoes. Add a dash of salt as needed. Cook for another two minutes, or until the stew comes up to a low simmer and is fully hot.

WHITE BEAN *and* ROSEMARY SOUP

Any soup that starts with canned beans sounds like a cheap-out, but this one is gloriously full of flavor because of the zing of the raw garlic, the earthy freshness of the rosemary, and the hint of umami from the Worcestershire. You can heft this up with a lot of things—greens like spinach or kale, meaty proteins like chopped ham or sausage, or the crunchy texture of croutons or panko. But I still love it as a silky smooth (and unintentionally vegan!) soup on its own, with a hunk of bread to scrape up all the extras.

Ingredients

2 15-oz (400 g) cans cannelloni beans (organic, low-sodium preferred)

1 large branch rosemary (or roughly 2 tablespoons)

4 tablespoons extra-virgin olive oil

4 garlic cloves

2 cups (450 mL / 16 oz) vegetable or chicken stock

2 teaspoons Worcestershire sauce

1 teaspoon Kosher salt (or more to your preference)

Dash of freshly ground pepper

Drain the beans (don't bother rinsing) and remove the rosemary from the branch. Add the beans and rosemary into a blender with the olive oil, garlic, stock, Worcestershire sauce, and salt. Blend, then heat—you can do this in your blender if it has a soup setting; you can transfer all the soup into a pot and heat on the stove; or you can heat in a large bowl or single servings in the microwave. Serve hot and top with the pepper and any additional toppings or additions you desire (see the headnote above).

BASIL PEA SOUP

Frozen peas are one of the greatest gifts—picked at the peak of freshness, they retain all the health benefits with none of the work. And since they are already cooked, you need to do very little to them to make them shine (although quality matters here, so make sure there are *no* additives, and organic is better if you can afford to do it). The raw garlic and fish sauce give the umami you'd normally get from the time-consuming step of caramelizing onions. Serve this cold or hot with a good crusty bread on the side for a meal you'd never guess was straight out of the freezer section.

Ingredients

20 oz (600 g) formerly frozen peas

Large bunch fresh basil, plus additional

2 cloves garlic

1 teaspoon fish sauce

Juice of 1 lime

3 cups (700 mL/24 oz) vegetable or chicken stock

4 dollops of crème fraiche (or Greek yogurt if you don't have it)

Chives (optional)

Sliced bread (optional)

Add the peas, basil, garlic, fish sauce, lime, stock, and crème fraiche to a blender and fully blend. You can serve this cold or pour it into a pot and bring it up to temperature. Top with chopped chives and serve with bread on the side.

COCONUT LENTIL SOUP

I love lentils, but I've always been a bit lazy about making them. Then I was introduced to canned lentils, and I gained one of my all-time favorite pantry additions. Lentils in soup add a heartiness that means you don't need to involve meat or rice or noodles, and the bonus is that this type of recipe works for almost every possible dietary restriction. You can sub in any easy veggie here—snap peas, spinach, or frozen peas, all would also do great, but I particularly love the texture of bok choy here. This soup is healthy, packed with flavor from the one-two punch of coconut milk and red curry paste, and, at less than ten minutes, it's one of the quickest ways to get a satisfying homemade meal on the table.

Ingredients

2 15-oz (400 g) cans of coconut milk

1 cup (250 mL/8 oz) water

4 tablespoons red curry paste

2 teaspoons Kosher salt

6 bunches baby bok choy

Large bunch basil

2 15-oz (400 g) cans of lentils

Sriracha (optional)

Put the coconut milk, water, red curry paste, and salt into a large pot on medium high heat.

While the liquid is coming up to a low simmer, roughly chop the bok choy (slice off the ends and then dice the stems as well as the leaves). Add it into the pot. Chop the basil and add that in too. Drain the lentils and then add them in as well. Let it all cook for around five minutes or until the bok choy has softened but still has a bit of crunch. Taste to see if you need more salt. Serve hot and add in sriracha if you prefer your soups a bit spicier.

LASAGNA SOUP

I, like most sentient beings, love lasagna. But I am also way too lazy to make it most of the time. You have to preheat an oven? And *layer things*? And then wait forever for it to cook? No thanks. This soup gives you all the flavor of lasagna without the work. It uses beef, but you could easily sub in chicken or pork (or even keep it vegetarian!) if you wanted. So break up your lasagna noodles and make lasagna a little easier on yourself, won't you?

Ingredients

Dash of extra-virgin olive oil

1 pound (16 oz / 454 g) ground beef

1 teaspoon Kosher salt, plus additional

2 tablespoons onion powder

2 tablespoons fresh oregano

1 large bunch basil

4 cups (1 L / 32 oz) chicken broth

1 28-oz (794 g) can crushed tomatoes

½ pound (227 g) lasagna noodles

½ pound (227 g / 8 oz) full-fat ricotta cheese, plus additional to dollop

Grated parmesan cheese

In a large pot on medium high heat, add the olive oil, beef, salt, and onion powder and combine. Let the meat cook for three minutes or until it has begun to brown.

While the beef is cooking (if you have time—you could also do this once the noodles are cooking), remove the oregano from the stems (you can use 2 teaspoons of dried oregano instead, if you need to, but fresh is very much preferred). Remove the basil from the stems as well (you can chop it if you'd like, but it isn't necessary).

Add the broth and tomatoes to the pot and increase the heat to high, so it comes to a boil quickly. Break up the lasagna noodles (into pieces about the size of large potato chips) and put them in the pot. Add in the oregano and basil as well as the ricotta. Stir, reduce the heat just a bit, and let the mixture lightly boil for around eight minutes, or until the noodles are cooked but al dente.

Remove from the heat, taste to see if you need more salt, and spoon into bowls, topping with another small dollop of ricotta as well as however much parmesan you like.

CHARRED ZUCCHINI SOUP

I adore the flavor that char adds, but you don't need a grill to make it happen. This recipe calls for just your plain old gas stove. Don't get scared of burning zucchini on a flame—trust the recipe, and you'll find the easiest way to make a complex, smoky soup without having to turn on an entire outdoor appliance.

Ingredients

5 medium zucchini

1 lemon

1 teaspoon Kosher salt, plus additional

Dash of pepper

1 garlic clove

½ cup (125 mL / 4 oz) olive oil

1 cup (250 mL / 8 oz) water or vegetable broth

Bread to serve (optional)

If you have a gas stove, then turn on two burners to medium high heat. Place the zucchini directly on top and cook for eight minutes, turning every two minutes or until charred on all sides. (If you do not have a gas stove, you can place the zucchini under the broiler in your oven, but be sure to turn every minute or so.)

While the zucchini is cooking, juice a lemon into a blender container. Add in the salt, some pepper, garlic, the olive oil, and the water/stock. Once the zucchini is cooked, add it in (cutting in half as needed, depending on the size and strength of your blender), and then blend everything together fully until the mixture is smooth. Taste to see if any additional salt or pepper is desired.

If needed, heat the soup up, either in a microwave for two to three minutes or on the stove until simmering. Serve hot and with bread or something additional on the side.

LOBSTER RAMEN

Throw out that flavor packet in your ramen and give yourself a similarly quick treat instead. Cooked lobster meat is an easy way to incorporate something special into an otherwise economical dish—and if you're not up for a splurge, there's even a fair amount of inexpensive imitation lobster you can find in the freezer section. Seafood stock has a richness that pairs perfectly with typical ramen flavors like soy and miso. And by adding simple extras like mushrooms and shelled edamame, you get a whole rounded meal without a lot of fuss.

Ingredients

6 cups (1.5 L/ 48 oz) seafood broth (lobster bouillon also works great)

⅓ cup (76 g/ 2.6 oz) miso paste

2 tablespoons sesame oil

2 tablespoons soy sauce

6 scallions

1 cup (88 g/ 3 oz) baby bella mushrooms (or other small mushroom)

8 oz (227 g) cooked lobster meat (or imitation lobster)

1 cup (150 g/ 5 oz) shelled edamame

12 oz (400 g) ramen noodles (or four individual ramen noodle blocks)

Dash of Kosher salt

In a large pot, bring the broth up to a high simmer and whisk in the miso paste, sesame oil, and soy sauce.

Chop the scallions and mushrooms and throw them in the broth. Allow to cook for two minutes. Chop the lobster if needed and then add the lobster, edamame, and ramen noodles into the pot (if your edamame is frozen, put that in first for a minute).

Cook for two to three minutes (or follow the ramen directions for timing). Taste to see if any additional salt is needed. Serve hot.

MISO NOODLE SOUP

Classic miso soup is something we think of as a treat at a Japanese restaurant, but it's deceptively simple to make a version at home. This is not anything close to traditional—dashi (or stock made from the seaweed kombu) is a more classic ingredient, but in lieu of that, you can still make something excellent. Instead, this dish is banking on the now-universal combo of miso paste and seaweed snacks. If you have access to dashi, then you can sub that in for the water to make an even more complex soup, but this recipe works for a weekday meal that will make you feel cozy in less than ten minutes and fill you up with the easy additions of tofu and noodles.

Ingredients

8 cups (2 L/64 oz) water or vegetable stock (or dashi, preferably, if you have it)

½ cup (115 g/4 oz) white miso paste

2 tablespoons soy sauce

Large handful of spinach

1 14-oz (397 g) package of firm tofu

½ pound (225 g/8 oz) thin rice noodles (quick-cooking ramen, egg, or wheat noodles also work fine)

5 grams (or around ½ cup when crumbled) dried seaweed snack

Salt to taste

Place the water or stock in a pot on high heat. Whisk in the miso paste and the soy sauce. While waiting for the liquid to come up to a boil, chop the spinach and cut the tofu into small bite-sized pieces.

When the liquid is at a boil, turn the heat down slightly and add in the spinach, tofu, and rice noodles. Let cook around three minutes, or according to package instructions. Crumble in the seaweed. Stir and then taste to see if any additional salt is needed. Serve immediately.

04

PASTA AND NOODLES

BUCATINI ALL'AMATRICIANA-ISH

Apologies in advance to any Italian person who wants to berate me for suggesting that the typical guanciale of this recipe can be replaced by pancetta. I completely agree that, if you can find the fatty, peppery pork jowl delight that is guanciale, by all means purchase it for this dish. But in the absence of that, cubed pancetta—a much more easily procured pork belly cut that needs no major cook time because it is cured—can serve in its place. And it would be such a shame not to have any version, because this is among the simplest yet most perfect dishes ever created. Passata is pureed and strained tomato sauce, so it leads to a thick and smooth sauce. The bucatini absorbs the sauce and the hint of spice from the chili and black pepper to make this irresistible.

Ingredients

1 pound (454 g / 16 oz) bucatini pasta

6 oz (175 g) cubed pancetta

2 cups (500 g) tomato passata (or 1 28-oz can of crushed tomatoes)

½ teaspoon dried red chili flakes

Heavy dash of fresh ground black pepper

Grated pecorino cheese

Bring a pot of heavily salted water to a boil. Add the bucatini and cook for approximately six minutes or until the bucatini is very al dente.

While the pasta is cooking, add the pancetta to a saucepan on medium high heat and cook for roughly two minutes. Add the tomato passata, chili flakes, and black pepper, and bring the sauce up to a heavy simmer.

When the bucatini is still very al dente, but still needs a minute or so of cooking time, drain it and add it into the sauce along with your preferred amount of grated pecorino. Stir the pasta as needed, and then serve hot once the bucatini is the right bite of al dente.

SESAME NOODLES

New Yorkers love their Chinese American food, and nothing feels more like the city's perfect hybrid than the classic sesame noodles. This version is a totally untraditional riff that utilizes tahini, since it is ubiquitous and gives the perfect simple sesame hit. Serve this hot or cold and have a quick simple meal that feels luxurious.

Ingredients

12 oz (40 g) thin noodles (ramen, somen, or a pasta like capellini work great)

¼ cup (60 mL/2 oz) rice vinegar (cider or white wine vinegars also work fine, but reduce the amount by half)

2 tablespoons soy sauce

1 tablespoon peanut butter

3 tablespoons tahini

1 bunch scallions

3 Persian cucumbers or 1 small English cucumber

1 tablespoon sesame seeds (optional)

Bring a pot of heavily salted water to a boil. Cook the noodles according to the directions (some might take as little as two minutes and others longer, so take that timing into account).

While your water is coming to a boil and/or noodles are cooking, make your sauce. Put the vinegar, soy sauce, peanut butter, and tahini in a bowl and fully combine. Chop the scallions and the cucumber.

When your noodles have finished cooking, drain them and add the chopped scallions, cucumbers, and sauce. Toss to combine. Top with the sesame seeds if you'd like, and serve.

WHITE WINE, GOAT CHEESE, *and* SPINACH PASTA

Five ingredients plus salt are all you need when you have the tangy softness of goat cheese paired with the crispness of a white wine. It's such a perfect sauce that it can work across a multitude of pasta shapes—so pick your favorite! It's simplicity at its best and a pasta everyone will want seconds of.

Ingredients

3 cups (750 mL/24 oz) water or broth (plus additional)

2 cups (250 mL/16 oz) dry white wine

Heavy dash of Kosher salt

1 pound (454 g/16 oz) pasta (whatever shape you prefer)

10 oz (280 g) spinach (frozen is fine if defrosted)

8 oz (226 g) goat cheese

Put the water/broth and wine into a wide pot and bring to a boil. Add the salt and pasta and cook, stirring occasionally. As the liquid reduces and the pasta cooks, add more water/broth as needed. (You shouldn't need much, though, so don't add too much! You can always add more, but it's harder to take out. And as you get toward the end, it's okay if there's only a little water left, as long as when you taste it, it tastes nearly done.)

After five minutes, add the spinach and cover, stirring every minute or so (the length of time will depend on the pasta you are cooking—make sure to keep checking in). About a minute from finishing, add the goat cheese, fully combine, and serve.

AMALFI LEMON PESTO PASTA

Italy's Amalfi Coast is known for its abundance of lemons. They're a different variety to the ones we find commonly here, but this lemon pesto is based on that vivid fantasy of sunshine, seaside, and lemony goodness. Try to get organic lemons if you can, because they tend to have more vibrant rinds.

Ingredients

2 large lemons	Ground black pepper
2 tablespoons parsley	Grated parmesan
1 pound (454 g/ 16 oz) angel hair pasta	Extra-virgin olive oil
1 teaspoon Kosher salt, plus additional	1 cup (92 g/ 3 oz) sliced almonds

Bring a pot of salted water to boil (try to add only as much as is needed to cover the pasta). While waiting, zest the lemons—get as much of the yellow rind, without getting any of the white pith, as you can. Chop the parsley and set aside.

Add the pasta to the boiling water and cook for the allotted time (typically around three to four minutes). Make the pesto: juice both lemons into a blender and add half the zest. Add the salt and freshly ground black pepper. Add a healthy pour of parmesan, olive oil, and half the almonds, and blend.

When the pasta is done cooking, drain it (but retain a bit of the pasta water, in case you want to loosen the sauce later). Add the pesto and the remaining zest and almonds into the pasta. Combine, adding in a dash of pasta water if needed. Taste to see if more salt or lemon is needed (depending on the size and juiciness of your lemons, you may want to add more). Top with the parsley, and an additional dash of fresh pepper.

CLAMS *and* FIDEOS

If you love paella but don't want to deal with rice, then I'd love to introduce you to the concept of fideos. While the Spanish have their own particular thin, short noodle, we can approximate here by breaking up a thin pasta. (I urge all my Spanish friends to note that I am emphatically pointing out that spaghetti is not real fideos, so please don't get upset.) But, as inauthentic as this recipe may be, the spirit of the flavors and delightful tiny noodles is alive. Combined with clams, you get a brothy, flavorful weeknight treat.

Ingredients

Heavy drizzle of extra-virgin olive oil

6 garlic cloves

1 pound (454 g/16 oz) spaghetti

24 small clams

2 tablespoons tomato paste

½ teaspoon smoked paprika

Dash of Kosher salt

5 cups (1.25 L/40 oz) chicken stock (plus any additional needed)

Large bunch of parsley

1 lemon

In a very large skillet or Dutch oven, heat the oil on medium heat. Chop up your garlic and rinse off your clams if they need it.

Break up the pasta into roughly one-inch pieces (these are the "fideos"). Add to the skillet and cook for two minutes, stirring frequently.

Add the tomato paste, garlic, paprika, and salt to the skillet and stir together. Add the clams and chicken stock and bring all to a boil. Cover and cook for six to eight minutes or until the clams have opened and the fideos have cooked. Stir every minute or so and add more broth if needed—the end result should have most of the broth soaked up, but you don't want to burn the bottom of the skillet.

While the fideos are cooking, chop the parsley and juice the lemon. When the fideos are ready, add the parsley and lemon. Serve hot.

ONE PAN *CACIO E PEPE*

This classic Roman dish is so uncomplicated that it is perfect—al dente pasta meets the tang of pecorino cheese and the hit of pepper that comes together with a few incredible ingredients. But that also means the ingredients themselves need to be good. Freshly grind your pepper. Buy a good pecorino and grate it yourself. Have a high-quality olive oil. Then the other trick is to make it all in one pan. The starchy water adds a beautiful texture and emulsifies the cheese. And the bonus is you have everything deliciously in one pot. This recipe is very light on the amounts, because who wants to measure out salt, olive oil, or freshly cracked pepper? Taste and add more as you go—it'll be much easier than handwringing over exact amounts in what is meant to be a rustic, easy dish.

Ingredients

5 cups (1.25 L/40 oz) water

Dash of Kosher salt

1 pound (454 g/16 oz) spaghetti

Pecorino Romano (enough for at least 1 cup/100 g when grated)

Heavy drizzle extra-virgin olive oil

Very heavy dash of freshly ground pepper (at least 2 teaspoons)

In a wide skillet (wide enough to lay your spaghetti flat), add the water along with a heavy dash of salt and bring it up to a boil. Add the spaghetti, making sure it is completely submerged (if it isn't, give it a minute to soften and then stir until it is). Let it continue at a high simmer, stirring occasionally as the pasta soaks up the water—you can start barely stirring, but watch it as it gets closer; you don't want the pasta to start sticking to the pan.

While the pasta is cooking, grate your pecorino. You want to grate it on the smallest holes possible on your box grater (or use a microplane)—the cheese is too hard to melt well otherwise, so you really want to make sure it is grated finely. You *can* buy pre-grated, but just please make sure it was grated that day and there are no additives in the cheese.

After seven to nine minutes (depending on your particular spaghetti), when the water is mostly absorbed into the pasta (but it's still a touch liquidy), turn the heat off. Add a heavy drizzle of olive oil. Crack lots of black pepper on top—this is a simple dish, and it does need a lot of pepper. Add in the cheese and combine. Add more salt or cheese to taste as desired.

ORECCHIETTE *with* SUNDRIED TOMATO *and* ARTICHOKE

This is one of those pantry stunners—it packs in more flavor than it has any right to. But because it is so simple, it lives and dies by its ingredients. Get good sundried tomatoes that are higher-quality and packed in oil; buy artichokes where you recognize all the ingredients in the marinade; spring for real Parmigiano Reggiano cheese. With better versions of each ingredient, you'll elevate the dish without any extra work on your end.

Ingredients

1 pound (454 g / 16 oz) orecchiette (or other small pasta)

Large bunch parsley

1 lemon

1 14-oz (400 g) jar of quartered marinated artichokes

½ cup (5 oz / 150 g) sundried tomatoes (preferably packed in oil)

Grated parmesan cheese

Heavy dash of Kosher salt

Bring a pot of salted water to a boil. Add the orecchiette and cook for seven to nine minutes, or until al dente.

While the pasta is cooking, prep the ingredients for the sauce and then add them into a bowl. Chop the parsley; zest the skin of the lemon; drain the artichokes (and chop them if you want but, if they're quartered, you don't have to); drain the sundried tomatoes of their liquid and then chop them. Juice a lemon into the bowl and then toss to combine with the chopped tomatoes, lemon zest, parsley, artichokes, cheese to your taste, and a heavy dash of salt.

When the pasta is done cooking, drain it, reserving a bit of the pasta water, and then combine with the sauce. Taste to see if you need any additional salt.

PASTRAMI SPICE BUCATINI

I know this is among the longest ingredient lists in this book, but you won't be sorry when you have this explosion of flavor—and it's really mostly just a matter of sticking a half teaspoon into a bunch of spices (and if you can't find a spice or two in your pantry, don't stress. It'll turn out fine). I love a pastrami sandwich, and this is like getting that in pasta form. It feels different without being hard and is delicious while also comforting. It's a hit with any crowd.

Ingredients

6 to 8 cups (1.5 to 2 L) beef broth

Dash of Kosher salt, plus additional

1 pound (454 g/16 oz) bucatini

Heavy drizzle of olive oil

½ teaspoon coriander

½ teaspoon fennel seeds

½ teaspoon smoked paprika

½ teaspoon onion powder

½ teaspoon brown mustard seeds

1 tablespoon Dijon mustard

1 pound (450 g/16 oz) sliced pastrami

1 cup (250 g/8 oz) sauerkraut

Bring 6 cups (1.5 L) of the broth to a boil (keep the rest, depending on your brand of bucatini—it may need a bit more). Add a heavy dash of salt and add the bucatini. Cook the bucatini for six to eight minutes (or according to the time on your packaging). Keep in mind that the broth can soak in faster than water, so check and stir every minute or two.

While the bucatini is cooking, place a small pan on medium high heat and add the olive oil. Add in the spices (coriander, fennel seeds, smoked paprika, onion powder, and mustard seeds) along with the mustard and allow to cook for three to four minutes, stirring occasionally, then remove from the heat. While the spices are cooking, roughly chop the pastrami. Add the pastrami and sauerkraut into the spices and stir to combine.

When the bucatini is cooked, drain the remaining broth (reserving a few tablespoons in case you need it) and add in the pastrami/sauerkraut/spice mixture along with another generous dash of salt. Combine and serve hot.

ZUCCHINI NOODLES *with* RICOTTA *and* MINT

There's a reason why zoodles became a craze—you can now often buy the pre-spiralized versions in your grocery store if you don't want to purchase the machine for yourself—because it's not only healthy, but it's an incredibly quick meal. That being said, you need a good sauce to accompany it, otherwise it just feels like you're eating a pile of zucchini instead of something as filling and rich as pasta. This version tries to do a lot with a little, and every single ingredient is pulling its weight. The richness of the ricotta gives creaminess, while the mint and lemon add brightness. But the real star is the tang and crunch of the salt and vinegar chips. Textures and flavors meld perfectly for a satisfying meal from only a few ingredients.

Ingredients

4 to 6 large zucchini (or 6 cups/48 oz zucchini noodles)

2 tablespoons mint

1 lemon

1 pound (454 g/16 oz) ricotta

Dash of Kosher salt

1 cup (150 g/6 oz) salt and vinegar chips (when crushed)

Place a large saucepan on medium high heat. If you're making the noodles yourself, use a spiralizer to make them. Finely chop the mint. In a bowl, juice the lemon, then add the ricotta, mint, and dash of salt. Add the zucchini to the pan and cook for approximately two minutes, or until the zoodles soften but still retain some bite. While the zoodles are cooking, crush the chips. Remove the pan from the heat, stir in the ricotta mixture, and top with the chips. Serve hot.

ASPARAGUS FUSILLI *with* PICKLED ONIONS *and* RICOTTA

This recipe *does* require three pots, but not a single one needs to be scrubbed at the end, so in my book it still definitely counts as a quick meal. And it's worth it because the gusto of the pickled onions melds so gorgeously with the creamy ricotta. It is soothing enough to make any weeknight feel a bit brighter.

Ingredients

1 ½ cups (375 mL/ 12 oz) cider vinegar (or as much as you need to cover the onions)

1 red onion

Dash of Kosher salt

Dash of sugar

1 pound (454 g/ 16 oz) fusilli

1 pound (454 g/ 16 oz) asparagus

Dash of extra-virgin olive oil

1 pound (454 g/ 16 oz) ricotta

Put a pot of salted water on to boil (make sure not to fill it up too much—you just need enough to cover the pasta, and the less water you have the faster it will heat up).

In a small pot, bring the vinegar up to a boil. Dice the red onion into small pieces. Add the onion to the boiling vinegar, along with a dash of salt and sugar, and mix well. Turn off the heat.

Add the fusilli to the boiling water and cook it according to the package time (usually about six to eight minutes).

Place a saucepan on high heat. Chop the asparagus. Add it into the saucepan with a dash of salt and olive oil—the pan should be hot enough to sizzle, you want the asparagus to char a bit. After around two to three minutes it should be cooked, and you can remove it from the heat.

When the pasta is ready, drain the water (but make sure to retain some of the pasta water so you can use it later). Drain the vinegar from the onion. Combine the pasta, onion, asparagus, and ricotta. Stir together, and if you want a more liquidy sauce, add a bit of pasta water. Serve hot.

SOY SAUCE BUTTER NOODLES

I'm not sure if you'll ever find a better combination than unsalted butter and soy sauce—the unctuous, umami, salty merger is unparalleled. And luckily, it couldn't be easier. This recipe adds a bright hit of chives on top of instant noodles to round everything out. We are lucky to live in a time when the quality of instant noodles is incredible—if you can seek out the Taiwanese brand A-Sha, which hand-cuts and air-dries its noodles, you'll be glad you did. But any store-brand instant noodle works great here too. As long as you have that perfect soy and butter combination, you will not be disappointed.

Ingredients

12 oz (400 g) ramen (or other instant, like A-Sha) noodles

Small bunch chives

4 tablespoons unsalted butter (European style like Kerrygold or Plugra preferred)

½ cup (125 mL / 4 oz) soy sauce

Juice of half a lemon

Bring a pot of salted water to a boil. Add the noodles and cook for two to three minutes, or until they are cooked but still a bit al dente. While the noodles are cooking, chop the chives.

When the noodles are done, drain the water immediately and throw the butter, soy sauce, and lemon onto the noodles. Combine fully, then add the chives on top. Serve hot.

BROCCOLI *and* ANCHOVY PASTA

My main reason for eschewing some frozen veggies is texture, but this recipe actually leans into that softness. Mashing up broccoli allows it to meld into a perfect sauce with the anchovies to give a healthy, flavorful treat. It's a quick fix that will also make you feel grateful you're getting veggies in without all the work.

Ingredients

1 pound (454 g / 16 oz) elbow pasta (or another small pasta)

1 pound (454 g / 16 oz) frozen broccoli florets

Dash of extra-virgin olive oil

6 cloves garlic

2 oz (55 g) anchovies, packed in oil

½ tablespoon red pepper flakes

1 lemon

Dash of Kosher salt

Bring a pot of salted water to a boil. Put a large saucepan on medium high heat.

When the water comes to a boil, add the pasta. Cook for five to six minutes or until the pasta is al dente and cooked through.

While the pasta is cooking, add the broccoli into the pan with a dash of olive oil. Mince the garlic and add it to the broccoli, along with another dash of olive oil, the anchovies (with their oil as well), and the red pepper flakes. Allow everything to cook for five minutes or so (it could be shorter or longer, depending on the size of the broccoli). When the broccoli softens, mash it with a masher (like what you'd use for mashed potatoes) and mix everything together. Let it keep cooking until the pasta is done.

When the pasta has cooked, drain it (retaining a small amount of pasta water). Add the broccoli mixture and juice the lemon on top. Stir together and taste to see if additional salt is needed (it almost certainly will be). Serve hot.

BLISTERED CHERRY TOMATO SPAGHETTI

Some combos are classic for a reason, and tomatoes and spaghetti can't be beat. This recipe enhances the basic by adding char to the tomatoes and a whole lot of garlic. I know the minimal ingredients might seem counterbalanced by using the stove, oven, and blender, but trust me it's worth it (and the cleanup is still pretty easy). You *can* use regular spaghetti here, but just keep in mind that it might take longer.

Ingredients

1 pound (454 g/16 oz) thin spaghetti

10 cloves garlic

3 cups (700 g/24 oz) small cherry tomatoes

Dash of olive oil, salt, and pepper

1 cup (100 g/8 oz) grated parmesan

Put a pot of salted water on to boil—make sure to only use as much water as you need to cover the pasta, so it heats up more quickly. Place an oven rack as close to the top as you can and turn on your broiler.

When the water starts to boil, add the spaghetti. A thin spaghetti should only take around five to six minutes to cook, so keep an eye on it. Drain when cooked.

While the spaghetti is cooking, smash the garlic. Line a sheet tray with foil and put the tomatoes and garlic on top, then sprinkle with olive oil, salt, and pepper. Put the sheet tray in the oven, right under the broiler. Cook for three to five minutes, or until the cherry tomatoes have begun to char (the timing will be very dependent on your broiler and the size of your cherry tomatoes, so don't be afraid to leave it longer as needed).

When the tomatoes are done, take the garlic and half the tomatoes and place them in a blender along with another dash of salt. Add the tomato sauce mixture and the remaining cherry tomatoes to the pasta and stir to combine. Add the parmesan and serve hot.

05

RICE BOWLS

SPICY TUNA RICE BOWL

I adore the simplicity of this version of tuna salad—it's an easy classic, but a few go-to ingredients make all the difference. The sriracha adds a dose of spice, the vinegar gives a welcome sweet blast of acidity, and the cornichons pack the perfect texture and flavor punch. Heat it up or eat it cold; either way, it'll become your easiest pantry meal.

Ingredients

½ cup (120 g/4 oz) cornichons

3 Persian cucumbers or 1 small English cucumber

4 cups (600 g/32 oz) cooked rice

4 5-oz (145 g) cans tuna (packed in oil preferred)

½ cup (170 mL/4 oz) mayonnaise

2 tablespoons sriracha

2 tablespoons white vinegar (or rice vinegar)

2 tablespoons black sesame seeds

Dash of Kosher salt

Dice the cornichons and the cucumbers. Heat up your rice in the microwave if you want to. In a bowl, combine the tuna, mayonnaise, sriracha, vinegar, and sesame seeds, and add in a dash of salt. Fold in the cornichons and cucumbers. Taste to see if any additional salt is needed. Top the rice with the tuna (either in one bowl or separated out into four bowls). Heat up for thirty seconds in the microwave if you desire.

THAI-INSPIRED BASIL CHICKEN
with SCALLIONS

There are few dishes as beloved as the classic Thai basil chicken. The herbaceousness of the abundant basil grounds the meaty umami of the rest of the flavors. If you can find Thai chilis and/or Thai basil, it really adds a lot of dimension to the dish, but it works just fine with whatever versions of herb and spice your grocery store can conjure.

Ingredients

1 pound (454 g/16 oz) ground chicken

3 tablespoons fish sauce

2 tablespoons soy sauce

1 teaspoon sugar

Dash of Kosher salt

16 oz (454 g) frozen green beans

1 Thai chili or small serrano pepper (optional)

4 scallions

3 garlic cloves

1 15-oz (400 g) can baby corn

2 bunches basil (Thai basil preferred)

4 cups (600 g/32 oz) cooked rice

In a wok or large saucepan, add the chicken, fish sauce, soy sauce, sugar, a dash of salt, and the green beans. Turn it on to medium high to high heat and let it start to cook. Stir every few minutes (the whole dish should cook in six to eight minutes total).

While the chicken is cooking, chop the chili/pepper if you are using it. Add it into the chicken mixture. Then chop the scallions and garlic cloves. Add them into the chicken mixture.

Drain the baby corn and add that into the chicken mixture. Take the basil leaves off of the stems and roughly rip them.

When the chicken is done, add the basil and remove the pan from the heat. Stir the basil in, top the chicken over the rice (you can microwave it to get it warm if you'd prefer), and serve hot.

CHICKEN LARB-ISH BOWL

I first had larb in Thailand and I was blown away—an abundance of herbs and greens counterbalances ground meat in a cacophony of flavor. This is not a traditional dish by any means, but the spirit of that abundance is in this dish. I love this as a filling rice bowl, but it also does well in other combinations like lettuce wraps or in pitas.

Ingredients

1 bunch spring onions

Dash of Kosher salt

Neutral oil like vegetable or canola

Small bunch mint

Small bunch cilantro

2 pounds (900 g/ 32 oz) ground chicken

2 tablespoons fish sauce

2 tablespoons soy sauce

2 limes

2 romaine heads

2 cups (300 g/ 16 oz) cooked rice

2 tablespoons sriracha (adjust to your preferred spice level)

Put a wok or large pan on medium high heat. Roughly cut the spring onions, place them in the pan, and add a dash of salt and oil.

Roughly chop the mint and cilantro (you need to remove the mint from the stems, but not the cilantro). Add half the herbs into the pan with the chicken, fish sauce, soy sauce, and juice of one lime. Stir to combine. Cook for at least two minutes.

While the chicken begins to cook, chop the romaine and then add it into the pan with the rice and sriracha. Combine and allow to cook until the chicken is no longer pink—it should be another two to four minutes. When finished, juice the remaining lime, throw in the rest of the herbs, and serve hot.

SALMON *and* GRAPEFRUIT POKE BOWL

It's no surprise poke bowls are popping up everywhere—why wouldn't everyone love the Hawaiian sushi-adjacent dish? The word poke means chunk in Hawaiian, but its meaning has expanded to most notably be associated with raw fish-topped rice bowls. This version is meant to be bright and a little bit different, with a one-two punch from the grapefruit and cilantro combination. Feel free to mix and match here however you want. Cucumbers or apple slices could give crunch instead of radishes; other leafy herbs like basil or parsley could step in for the cilantro; other citrus could sub in for grapefruit. But I personally love this combination and its surprising but delicious flavors.

Ingredients

1 bunch small radishes

1 pound (454 g/16 oz) sushi-grade salmon

Small bunch cilantro

1 large grapefruit

½ cup (125 mL/4 oz) soy sauce

Dash of Kosher salt

2 cups (300 g/16 oz) cooked rice (sushi rice is great, but not necessary if white rice is easier)

5 g (usually one snack pack) of seaweed snack

Dice the radishes. Slice the salmon into one-inch chunks. Chop the cilantro. Peel the grapefruit and then cut into one-inch chunks.

Place the radishes, salmon, cilantro, and grapefruit in a bowl. Toss with the soy sauce and a dash of salt.

Top the rice with the salmon mixture—you can either do one large bowl or split it between four separate bowls. Taste to see if you have enough salt. Crumble the seaweed on top. Serve cold.

CHILI GINGER SHRIMP FRIED RICE

Few combinations pack as much punch as sriracha and ginger—without much work, you can build entire worlds of flavor with just those two ingredients. But add in the delicate meatiness of shrimp, the canvas of rice, and a few other supporting ingredients, and you have a recipe you'll keep coming back to.

Ingredients

- 1 tablespoon olive oil
- 1 stalk ginger root (to make 1 teaspoon grated ginger)
- 1 pound (454 g/16 oz) peeled shrimp
- Dash of Kosher salt
- 1 tablespoon garlic powder
- 8 spring onions
- 1 cup (140 g/5 oz) frozen peas
- 2 lemons
- 4 cups (600 g/32 oz) cooked rice
- 2 teaspoons sriracha

Put the olive oil in a large saucepan and turn it on to medium high heat.

While the olive oil is heating up, peel the ginger root with a spoon and then grate it (alternately, if you want to use pre-minced ginger or ginger paste, that's okay in a pinch, but just don't use ginger powder here). Add the shrimp to the hot pan along with the dash of salt and half the garlic powder. Allow to cook for at least four minutes, stirring once halfway through.

While the shrimp is cooking, chop the spring onions. Add the spring onions, peas, juice of one lemon, the remaining garlic powder, and the ginger to the shrimp and cook for a minute. Add the rice, sriracha, additional lemon, and another dash of salt and cook for one more minute, or until the rice is hot.

CHAAT MASALA LEMON RICE BOWL

When I lived in India, I became obsessed with the roadside stands that sell savory snacks—or chaats—pretty much everywhere. One of the standard ingredients is the aptly named chaat masala. It's a spice blend that brings any dish alive with tang, funk, warmth, and depth. The main ingredient is dried mango powder (amchoor), but each blend is unique, with an array of spices like cumin, chili, ginger, pepper, salt, and coriander. Seek it out—even if your local grocery store doesn't have it, I promise it's only a two-day ship away. I sprinkle it on fruit, on sandwiches, into yogurt and even on toast. This vegetarian rice bowl sings with a bit of chaat masala and extra acidity from lemons. And in an ode to those puffed rice street snacks, I've topped it off with our American equivalent.

Ingredients

Drizzle of olive oil

Dash of Kosher salt

16 oz (454 g) frozen green beans

2 lemons

1 tablespoon chaat masala (or garam masala with tamarind paste in a pinch)

4 cups (600 g/32 oz) cooked rice

2 14-oz (400 g) cans chickpeas

1 cup (30 g) puffed rice cereal (like Rice Krispies)

Place a large skillet or wok on high heat. Add a drizzle of olive oil, a dash of salt, the green beans, juice of 1 lemon, and the chaat masala. Stir together for about a minute, then add the rice.

While the rice mixture is cooking, drain the chickpeas. Add the chickpeas into the skillet, along with the juice of the remaining lemon. Cook everything for another minute, or until the mixture is hot. Taste for whether you need more salt, and then top with the puffed rice cereal. Serve hot.

MICROWAVE STEAMED SALMON *with* GREEN BEANS

Salmon is one of our most beloved types of fish, but it is usually considered well outside the bounds of a 15 minute meal—you need to preheat an oven and give it enough time to cook through. But I started wondering if maybe we were giving the microwave short shrift. And sure enough, salmon does beautifully in the microwave, as long as you keep a few factors in mind to ensure it doesn't dry out. Even if you are not a big mayonnaise person, don't be afraid to use it here—it keeps everything moist, and it doesn't taste particularly mayo-ey with all the lemon and basil. Second, make sure your dish is completely covered so it steams and no moisture is released. If you're averse to a pinker salmon inside (something I wish everyone would accept as much as they accept medium rare beef), try to purchase a less thick cut of salmon. If you keep these small factors in mind, you'll be shocked at how well this simple dish turns out.

Ingredients

Small bunch of basil

2 lemons

Dash of Kosher salt

4 tablespoons mayonnaise

2 cups (300 g/ 16 oz) cooked rice

16 oz (454 g) frozen green beans

4 pieces of skinless salmon fillets
(on the thinner side if possible)

Tear the basil. In a small bowl, juice the lemons. Add in the mayonnaise and combine. Stir in the basil and a dash of salt.

Spread the rice across a microwaveable casserole dish. Pour a bit of the sauce on top, along with another dash of salt. Add the green beans, and pour on a bit more of the sauce and another dash of salt. Brush the salmon on both sides with the remaining sauce and salt as well.

Cover the casserole dish with parchment paper (keep it long enough to tuck in on both sides, so the dish can be completely contained—this is key, so that the salmon steams rather than getting overcooked if the moisture leaks out). Place in the microwave and cook for five minutes (add a minute if your salmon is particularly thick, but otherwise five minutes should be enough *unless*—and this is the big caveat—you have a microwave that isn't as powerful). The salmon should still be a little pink in the center when it is done.

SPICY TAHINI *and* TURKEY RICE BOWL

Turkey gets a bad rap apart from Thanksgiving, but it's great when you want something meaty that holds flavor. The secret is to keep it moist, and the tahini brings the creaminess while the hot sauce brings the spice. This is one of those eminently switchable recipes—you can throw in vegetable leftovers to the proceeding and the sauce combination will welcome all comers.

Ingredients

2 pounds (900 g/32 oz) ground turkey

2 tablespoons hot sauce

1 tablespoon garlic powder

Dash of Kosher salt

5 oz (142 g) spinach

2 bunches scallions

4 cups (600 g/32 oz) cooked rice

½ cup (115 g/4 oz) tahini

2 lemons

Place a large skillet or wok on high heat. Add the turkey with the hot sauce, garlic powder, and a dash of salt (start with at least half a teaspoon—I like up to a whole teaspoon of salt in this, but it depends on your preference). Mix together and then add the spinach. Stir occasionally, and cook for around three to five minutes or until the turkey starts to brown.

While the turkey is cooking, slice the scallions. Add the scallions into the skillet along with the rice and tahini. Mix fully. Allow to cook for another three to five minutes, or until the turkey is cooked through. Squeeze the lemons into the skillet and combine. Taste for whether you need more salt or hot sauce, and then serve hot.

06

SEAFOOD MEALS

SPICY TOMATO POACHED SHRIMP

This is one of those stewy one-pot meals that comes together incredibly quickly but feels like it contains more flavor than it has any right to. Harissa—the spicy, smoky North African red pepper condiment—forms the base layer, and it adds just the right level of heat. If you can't track it down (even though it is now widely available), you can always use your preferred hot sauce, and the rest of the ingredients will still pull their weight. Between the peppers, the chickpeas, and the shrimp, you've got an entire meal in a single serving.

Ingredients

2 red bell peppers

2 pounds (900 g/32 oz) peeled shrimp

2 tablespoons harissa

2 28-oz (794 g) cans of diced tomato

2 15-oz (400 g) cans of chickpeas

1 cup (180 g/6 oz) pitted kalamata olives

8 oz (227 g) feta

Dash of Kosher salt

Place a wok (or large Dutch oven) on high heat. Chop the bell peppers into bite-sized pieces. Throw half the bell peppers and all the shrimp into the wok with the harissa on top. Cook for three to four minutes without stirring, or until the shrimp have browned a bit. If you need to open your cans of tomatoes and chickpeas, do that now. Drain the chickpeas. If you prefer your olives chopped, you can also do that (but you don't have to).

Add the remaining bell peppers, the tomatoes, the chickpeas, and the olives to the wok. Cook for another five to six minutes, or until the shrimp have cooked through. Turn off the heat, crumble the feta in, and stir. Taste, then add some salt as needed. Serve hot.

BLACK PEPPER SHRIMP *and*
FETA LETTUCE WRAPS

This recipe is a pop of brightness on a plate. The spiciness of black pepper is the perfect pair with sweet shrimp, and I love letting the ingredients shine through the conduit of an easy lettuce wrap. Keep in mind that this is a messy, dribbly affair. You'll want a lot of napkins on hand, but you'll be hard-pressed to stop yourself from licking your fingers.

Ingredients

Dash of olive oil

1 pound (450 g/ 16 oz) peeled shrimp

1 teaspoon black pepper

1 teaspoon coriander

1 cup (100 g/ 8 oz) shredded carrots

Dash of Kosher salt

1 lime

1 head lettuce for wraps (butter, Boston, or iceberg work well)

8 oz (227 g) feta

Place a pan on medium high heat and add a dash of olive oil. Dice the shrimp into small pieces. Add the pepper and coriander to the shrimp. Add the shrimp to the pan. Cook for three to four minutes until the shrimp are cooked, or are no longer opaque and have turned pink. Remove from the heat, add the carrots and salt, then juice the lime on the shrimp. Add the shrimp mixture to each piece of lettuce, crumble a bit of feta on top, and wrap together to serve.

SHRIMP and BLACK BEANS with KALE and LIME

I love a simple greens and beans recipe—you just throw everything into a wok and cook until finished. It's really that simple! Kale, collards, escarole, spinach, and Swiss chard can all be used fairly interchangeably here (some wilt more than others and all have their own flavor, but they work well across many things). This one feels special because of the addition of shrimp, but peeled shrimp cook so quickly that they are an easy added bonus.

Ingredients

2 bunches kale

Olive oil

Dash of Kosher salt

1 tablespoon garlic powder

2 pounds (900 g / 32 oz) peeled shrimp

2 limes (or 3 if your limes are particularly small or not juicy)

2 15-oz (400 g) cans of black beans

Place a large wok or Dutch oven on high heat. Chop the kale. Add the kale to the wok and drizzle olive oil on top (if it's too much for your wok, you can let some cook down a little bit first to make room). Cook for two minutes or until the kale starts the wilt, stirring occasionally.

While the kale is cooking, add a dash of salt and the garlic powder. Add the shrimp to the wok. Then squeeze the juice of one lime onto the mixture. Let the shrimp cook for three to five minutes, or until almost ready.

While the shrimp is cooking, drain the black beans. Add them to the shrimp and kale mixture and then cook for another minute to bring the beans up to temperature. Squeeze the final lime juice on top and serve.

CLAM *and* CORN HASH BROWNS

I like to think of this dish as a deconstructed clam chowder—it's a one-pot wonder of surprising, filling, unctuous flavor that wonderfully doesn't need to cook any more than just heating it up. I know it might seem counterintuitive to have a meal where almost everything starts frozen or canned, but this really speaks to the quality you can find in both categories now. Get a good, sustainable canned clam and find organic frozen vegetables, and you'd never guess this was anything other than a fresh meal.

Ingredients

1 pound (450 g / 16 oz) frozen hash browns

1 pound (450 g / 16 oz) frozen corn

1 tablespoon smoked paprika

1 tablespoon onion powder

3 tablespoons butter

4 scallions

6 oz Canadian bacon
(around six thick slices)

10 oz (284 g) canned clams

Place a large wok or Dutch oven on high heat. Add the hash browns and corn and let cook for three to six minutes (timing will depend on how frozen they are). While cooking, add the paprika, onion powder, and butter.

Chop the scallions and throw them in as well, stirring occasionally. Cut the Canadian bacon into bite-sized pieces and add that in as well.

Drain the clams and add those in last, once everything feels mostly cooked through. Cook for an additional minute or two and then serve hot.

MISO MUSSELS *with* BOK CHOY

Mussels fulfill everything we want in a quick dinner—they cook fast, have a ton of flavor on their own, and are among the most inexpensive proteins around. So why do we only cook them for a special occasion? I think, once we get over our fear of the fanciness of mussels, we open up a whole new simple option. This recipe uses miso paste and garlic to amp up the flavor and pair it with the equally quick-cooking bok choy to make a whole meal in one pot, as simple as can be.

Ingredients

1 ½ cups (375 mL / 12 oz) vegetable or chicken broth

4 tablespoons white miso paste

1 tablespoon garlic powder

2 limes

Dash of Kosher salt

4 pounds (1.8 kg) mussels

4 large heads of baby bok choy

Crusty bread for serving (optional)

Place a very large pot on medium heat and add the broth, miso paste, and garlic powder. Juice the limes into the sauce as well, then whisk everything together. Taste and add salt as needed (with the miso paste and the broth, you may not need much, or even any).

Turn the heat up to medium high. While the sauce comes up to a heavy simmer, rinse off your mussels if needed. Then cut the ends off your bok choy and roughly chop into bite-sized pieces. Add the mussels, then the bok choy, to the pot and cover. Cook for three to five minutes, or until the mussels have opened. Stir to coat everything in the sauce. Serve immediately, with some crusty bread on the side to soak up the sauce.

MUSSEL *and* TOMATO RICE CAKE TOAST

We've all accepted a slice of bread as a conduit for a meal (hello, avocado toast), but why aren't we utilizing rice cakes in the same way? They have a texture and sturdiness that bread doesn't have—not to mention they make any gluten-avoiders happy. This recipe is eminently swappable. Use different seafood (if you can't find tinned mussels, then clams or oysters or even fish also work great. And don't worry if your mussels have flavors like paprika or are pickled—find the versions you like and use those flavors to your advantage); change up the veggies or herbs; heck, you can even add avocado and get in the millionth version of avocado toast. Either way, you'll become a rice cake toast convert in no time.

Ingredients

1 tablespoon tarragon

1½ cups (350 g/12 oz) cherry tomatoes

4 oz (110 g) cream cheese

1 tablespoon tomato paste

1 teaspoon salt (plus additional)

8 rice cakes

8 oz (200 g) tinned mussels

Take the tarragon off the stems. Halve the cherry tomatoes (or quarter if they are especially large).

In a bowl, combine the cream cheese, tomato paste, salt, and tarragon. Spread the cream cheese mixture onto the rice cakes. Drain the mussels of any oil they are packed in and then place them on top of the rice cakes. Add the tomatoes on top with an additional dash of Kosher salt.

ANCHOVY, BUTTER, *and* CAPERS *on* TOAST

When I first went to Italy, I couldn't believe the simplicity and reverence with which anchovies were served. Often you find them on their own, fanned across a plate. But on other occasions they are paired with good butter and bread. There's something about the brine with the cream with the dough that makes this combo utterly irresistible. But make sure you're seeking out a good anchovy and purchasing good butter. This recipe's uncomplicated setup relies on each ingredient standing out.

Ingredients

One loaf of crusty bread

4 tablespoons room-temperature butter (high-fat European butter like Kerrygold or Plugra preferred)

3 oz (55 g) anchovies, packed in oil (try for a higher-quality brand like Ortiz or Metro)

4 tablespoons capers

Dash of flaky sea salt

Slice the bread. Spread the butter on the bread. Top the butter with the anchovies, then the capers, then finish with a dash of salt.

SEARED TUNA *with* ENDIVE *and* ORANGE

Nothing cooks faster than a tuna steak, but it needs some heft to go along with it. Sweet oranges, salty soy sauce, briny olives, and bitter endive make for the perfect quick combination to hit every note with very little work. The key here is to not be afraid of higher heat, and to make sure you have fresh tuna that can be at its best when it's on the rarer side. If you have a large griddle pan, you could even make everything all at once other than the sauce. Who wouldn't like a meal special enough to serve to guests in only five minutes?

Ingredients

⅓ cup (83 mL/2.6 oz) soy sauce

2 large oranges (Valencia preferred)

4 endives

1 cup (180 g/6 oz) pitted Castelvetrano olives

Dash of Kosher salt

4 fillets of tuna (not too thick)

Place a nonstick griddle pan (or two large nonstick pans) on high heat. Separately, in a small pot, add the soy sauce and the juice of one of the oranges. Turn the heat onto medium high and bring to a boil. Once it's boiling, you can turn down the heat a bit, but don't turn it off—you want the sauce to reduce.

Cut the ends off the endives and chop them into quarters. Cut the other orange into slices—either peel it and cut the segments or (if it is an orange that is hard to peel) just slice off the ends. Put the endive, olives, and oranges on top of the griddle and let them cook for a minute or two, until they have charred. While those are cooking, salt the tuna heavily on both sides.

Remove the endive, oranges, and olives from the pan and put the tuna on. Cook on each side for one to three minutes, depending on how rare you want your tuna to be. When the tuna is cooked, combine with the endives, oranges, and olives and pour the soy-orange sauce on top. Serve hot.

THAI-INSPIRED FISH CURRY

I know most fish curries usually include a number of ingredients we are eschewing here—onions, garlic, and ginger most notably. But with the power of now readily available ingredients like Thai red curry paste, tamarind, and fish sauce, you can get a powerful punch without those seemingly essential staples. You can throw any vegetables in here (especially pre-cooked and chopped frozen ones), but I love the crunch and sweetness that bell peppers bring, and adding a green to the proceedings makes it feel heftier. It's a quick meal, but it packs a lot of flavor in.

Ingredients

½ cup (125 mL / 4 oz) tamarind paste/concentrate (or lime juice if you can't find tamarind)

1 13.5-oz (400 mL) can coconut milk

3 tablespoons Thai red curry paste

1 teaspoon brown sugar

1 teaspoon salt, plus additional

2 tablespoons fish sauce

2 limes

2 pounds (900 g / 32 oz) white fish like cod, haddock, or grouper

2 red or yellow bell peppers

5 oz (142 g) bok choy leaves or spinach

3 cups (450 g / 24 oz) cooked rice

1 bunch basil

Add the tamarind paste, coconut milk, red curry paste, brown sugar, salt, fish sauce, and juice of the limes to a large saucepan and place on medium heat. Whisk to combine.

While the sauce is heating up, cut the fish into one-inch pieces and dice the bell peppers. Add the fish and bell peppers to the pot, along with the bok choy leaves/spinach. Cover and cook for five minutes, or until the fish is cooked through.

While the fish is cooking, heat up your rice if you want, and roughly chop the basil. When the curry is finished cooking, taste and add salt as needed. Serve on the rice and top with the basil.

TAHINI LEMON FISH *over* CHARRED KALE

This is a simple one-pan meal that is as healthy as it is delicious. Tahini and lemon is one of my favorite combinations—it can do no wrong, and here it is the star, making sure the kale and fish shine.

Ingredients

3 lemons

⅓ cup (83 mL/2.6 oz) tahini

4 tablespoons olive oil

2 bunches of kale (or around 1 pound/450 g)

Dash of Kosher salt

4 fillets of a white flaky fish, like cod or haddock

Large handful of pine nuts

Turn on your oven's broiler. Line a sheet tray with aluminum foil.

In a small bowl, whisk together the juice of 2 lemons, the tahini, and the olive oil. Roughly chop the kale and then place in another bowl. Toss the kale with about two-thirds of the tahini lemon sauce, and then sprinkle a dash of salt on top. Put the kale on the sheet tray and then place the fish fillets evenly apart on the bed of kale. Drizzle the remaining sauce on top, along with more salt.

Place in the oven for six to seven minutes, or until almost cooked through. Throw the pine nuts on and squeeze the final lemon on top for the last minute. Remove from the oven and serve hot.

FLOUNDER *with* PISTACHIO PESTO *and* COUSCOUS

I know it's against the cardinal rule of 15 minute meals to have three dishes to clean at the end, but hear me out: this is such a crowd-pleasing delight that you won't mind the blender/pot/pan combo. Pistachio pesto with a lot of garlic gives a ton of flavor, and the thin meatiness of flounder is its perfect pair. Serve it with some pesto-ed up couscous, and you've got a dinner you could serve to guests or have as a healthy weeknight meal.

Ingredients

1 lemon

1 bunch basil

½ cup (120 mL/4 oz) olive oil, plus additional

6 cloves garlic

½ cup (70 g) pistachios

¼ cup (25 g/2 oz) grated parmesan cheese

1 teaspoon Kosher salt, plus additional

10 oz (284 g) formerly frozen peas

1 cup (150 g/8 oz) couscous

4 flounder fillets

Bring 2 cups of water to a boil in a small pot (you can do this on the stovetop or in the microwave). Place a wide saucepan on medium high heat (it should be large enough to fit the four fish fillets with space in between).

Add the couscous, a dash of salt, and the peas to the boiling water, cover, remove from heat, and let sit for around five minutes.

In a blender, combine the juice of the lemon with the basil, olive oil, garlic, pistachios, cheese, and salt.

Add a dash of oil to the pan. Rub about half the pesto around the fish, making sure it's heavy on one side. Place the fish on the pan (heavy-pesto side down) and let cook for two minutes. Then flip and cook one additional minute.

Add the remaining pesto into the couscous and combine with a fork. Serve the fish on top of the couscous.

SPICY CRAB TACOS

Crab and crunch go together perfectly, and this recipe is one of the quickest ways to a spicy, crunchy, meaty no-cook meal. Tacos are the easiest conduit, but with a bit of heat and lemon on your side, you'll find these to be as flavor-packed as you might expect.

Ingredients

2 avocados

2 lemons

1 small bunch cilantro

2 cups (450 g/16 oz) lump crab meat

1 cup (100 g/8 oz) shredded carrots

1 ½ tablespoons sriracha (or more or less depending on your preferred spice level)

Dash of Kosher salt

8 to 12 taco shells or tortillas

Slice the avocados into bite-sized pieces and spoon them into a bowl. Juice the lemons into the bowl. Chop the cilantro and add it into the bowl along with the crab, carrots, sriracha, and dash of salt. Stir to combine, then add the mixture to the taco shells or tortillas.

COD *in* GINGER LIME BROTH

Poaching fish is one of the easiest and most tender ways to cook it. And this recipe takes the very mild cod and gives it a barrage of flavor with ginger, soy, and basil. Add in quick-cooking snap peas, spinach, and tomatoes, and you've got a meal in minutes. This also goes great with a hunk of bread on the side to dip in the sauce and make the meal a bit heftier.

Ingredients

4 cups (1 L/32 oz) vegetable broth

2 limes (or, if they aren't particularly juicy, 3)

1 knob, about a tablespoon, of ginger (skin on)

2 tablespoons soy sauce

4 large basil leaves, plus additional

1 teaspoon salt, plus additional

4 fillets of cod, or other thick white fish

2 cups (250 g) snow peas

5 oz (142 g) spinach

1 ½ cups (350 g/12 oz) cherry tomatoes

Place the broth in a wide Dutch oven or deep saucepan. Turn up to medium heat and cover. While the broth is heating up, add the juice of the limes, the ginger, soy sauce, basil, and salt into a blender and blend. Then add the mixture into the broth.

When the broth is simmering, add the cod. Cook for five to seven minutes, or until it is almost cooked through and flaky.

While the cod is cooking, roughly chop the snap peas (you really don't need to trim them). Add the snap peas, tomatoes, and spinach into the broth. Cook until finished, another minute or two, and then taste to see if any additional salt is needed. Serve hot.

07

MEATY
MEALS

TURMERIC YOGURT CHICKEN *with* CASHEWS *and* CUCUMBER

I lived in India for a year, and one of the dishes I came away obsessed with was tandoori chicken. The tang of yogurt, citrus, and spices is unbeatable—and a great base, even if you don't have your own tandoor oven. This recipe uses chicken thighs, since they have the most flavor. Keep in mind that cutting chicken into chunks in a relatively quick way requires a sharp knife—so either sharpen those knives or buy your chicken pre-chopped.

Ingredients

Neutral oil such as canola or vegetable

1 cup (250 g/8 oz) Greek yogurt

1 tablespoon turmeric

1 teaspoon cumin

2 teaspoons Kosher salt

2 limes

2 pounds (900 g/32 oz) boneless chicken thighs

4 Persian cucumbers (or 1 large English)

1 cup (140 g) cashews

1 15-oz (400 g) can chickpeas

Place a large pan or Dutch oven on medium high heat and drizzle on some vegetable or canola oil.

In a bowl, combine the yogurt, turmeric, cumin, salt, and the juice of 1 lime. Cut the chicken thighs into bite-sized pieces and then toss the chicken in the yogurt sauce. Add the chicken into the pan and cook, stirring occasionally. The chicken will take around four to six minutes to cook.

While the chicken is cooking, dice the cucumbers. Toss the cucumbers, cashews, and chickpeas in the empty yogurt bowl and toss to cover with whatever yogurt remains. When the chicken is about one minute out from being done, add the cucumbers, cashews, and chickpeas to the pan. Cook until everything is hot and serve.

GROUND CHICKEN PICCATA

I love the flavors of chicken piccata—zingy lemon matched with the pickled delight of capers—but it doesn't have to always include a long bout of dredging raw chicken in flour. This version takes all of the gusto and none of the hassle by using ground chicken. To make it a full meal, I like to serve it over fast-cooking couscous, but if you're trying to avoid grains, serve over kale or spinach—or you can even throw the greens into the pot. It's a one-stop flavor vehicle.

Ingredients

2 pounds (900 g / 32 oz) ground chicken

1 teaspoon Kosher salt

1 cup (150 g / 8 oz) couscous

3 lemons

Small bunch parsley

3 tablespoons room-temperature butter

¼ cup (57 g / 2 oz) capers

Set a pot with 1 ¼ cups water to boil. Place a nonstick saucepan or wok on medium high heat. Add the chicken to the pan with one teaspoon of salt (and if you aren't sure about how nonstick your pan is, add a touch of neutral oil as needed).

When the water is boiling, add the couscous, another dash of salt, and the juice of 1 lemon. Remove from the heat, cover, and let sit for five minutes. In the meantime, lightly chop the parsley.

Don't move the meat for three to five minutes, or until it has browned on one side. Once it has, break it up fully and then add the butter, capers, juice of 1 more lemon, and the parsley. Let the chicken cook for another minute, or until it has just cooked through—be very careful here to not overcook. Since it has already browned on one side, it just takes a little bit more to cook, and since it is ground meat, it can overcook quickly.

Remove the chicken from the heat and squeeze the last lemon on top. Serve the chicken on top of the couscous (or greens if you'd prefer).

CHICKEN SAUSAGE *and* ARTICHOKES *over* POLENTA

This is a dish that is almost entirely from the pantry, and yet it couldn't feel more vibrant—and it's so easy that it's really more about heating up than actual cooking. Sausages and artichokes are well known staple pantry heroes, but I wish pre-made polenta got more attention. It adds heft the way that pasta or rice might to a dish, but it is incredibly simple and gives a nutty corn element. And all together with that hit of sumac, you get a dish that will make everyone crave seconds.

Ingredients

Drizzle of olive oil

24 oz (680 g) of chicken sausages

2 14-oz (400 g) cans marinated quartered artichoke hearts

1 tablespoon sumac

Dash of Kosher salt

16 oz (500 g) polenta roll

Small bunch parsley

Grated parmesan

Heat a heavy dollop of olive oil in a wide saucepan over medium high heat. Chop the sausage into bite-sized pieces and add them into the pan. Cook for around two minutes without stirring, until they begin to brown.

Drain the artichoke hearts. Add the artichokes, sumac, and dash of salt to the pan and stir. Cook for another two minutes.

While the sausage is cooking, slice the polenta into one-inch rounds. Remove the sausage mixture from the pan and add the polenta, sprinkling another dash of salt on top. Let the polenta cook for two minutes, or until it begins to brown, and then flip over, salt again, and cook for another two minutes.

While the polenta is cooking, chop the parsley. When it is ready, add the sausage mixture back on top of the polenta, and sprinkle the parsley and a heavy dose of parmesan on top. Cover and cook for another minute. Serve hot.

CHICKEN *and* OLIVE COUSCOUS

Simplicity among crowd-pleasers is the key to this recipe. Briny olives meld with the meatiness of the chicken. Thinly sliced chicken breasts can actually retain their moisture while getting a bit of a char with the broiler—it's the secret to flavorful chicken every time. Top with herbs to round everything out.

Ingredients

2 cups (500 mL/ 16 oz) chicken broth

1 pound (454 g/ 16 oz) thin sliced chicken breast

Extra-virgin olive oil

Kosher salt

2 cups (300 g/ 16 oz) couscous

1 cup (180 g/ 6 oz) large green pitted olives, Castelvetrano preferred

Medium bunch of parsley

½ cup (46 g/ 1.5 oz) sliced almonds

Make sure your top rack is only four inches from the top and turn on your broiler. In a pot, bring the broth to a boil with a dash of salt.

Place chicken breasts on a sheet tray, and oil and salt them on both sides. Put them in the oven for six minutes, turning at three minutes.

While the chicken is cooking, add the couscous to the pot, stir, cover, and turn the heat off. Chop the olives as well as the parsley. Then chop up the chicken once it is out of the oven. Fluff the couscous with a fork and then add the olives, almonds, and chicken. Mix together and top with the parsley.

ITALIAN SAUSAGE BURGER *with* QUICK PICKLED RED ONIONS

Why should beef get to have all the fun? Italian sausage makes a great patty base for a burger, and with a few quick condiments, you can have a combination that feels exciting and elevated without all the work. Sliced red onions get that delightfully acidic pickle flavor with only about five minutes of sitting in vinegar—so they are the perfect accompaniment to a 15 minute meal that you want to make feel a bit more exciting. I like adding the silky earthiness of the roasted red peppers and the subtlety of provolone, but this is another one of those recipes that also does great with a mix-and-match.

Ingredients

Extra-virgin olive oil

Kosher salt

2 pounds (900 g/32 oz) Italian sausage (hot, sweet, or mild is up to you!)

1 small red onion

1 cup (250 mL/8 oz) cider vinegar

½ cup (75 g/2.6 oz) of jarred roasted red peppers (preferably in liquid)

6 oz (170 g) sliced provolone cheese

4 to 6 buns

Heat up a grill or large grill pan on medium high heat (you can also use a regular pan in a pinch) with a light layer of olive oil. Add a dash of salt to the sausage. (You can also add herbs like dried oregano or basil, but it depends on how seasoned your sausage already is, so make it to your taste. A good Italian sausage shouldn't need it.) Form 4 to 6 patties from the meat—you can make them as large or small as you want—but just keep in mind that you do want it to cook through (and quickly), so you want them to be thinner than your average beef patty and flatter than you usually would make them (like a smashed burger).

Place the patties on top of the grill or grill pan. Cook four to five minutes on each side, depending on how large your patties are, flipping halfway through.

While the sausage patties are cooking, slice the red onion into rings. You want them to be fairly thin, but it doesn't matter much (rather, you want to just get it done). Break the rings apart and put them in a bowl with the cider vinegar and another dash of salt. Make sure the rings are fully submerged (you can add more cider vinegar as needed). Let them sit for at least five minutes.

When the patties are about one minute from being done, flip them again so the hot side is facing up. Add some of the peppers, then a heavy dose of red onion, and then top with a slice or two of the provolone cheese. Remove from the heat and place on the buns. Serve hot.

SOY SEAWEED PORK CHOPS

I've always thought that roasted seaweed snacks are perfection—they are like healthy, easy, shelf-stable delights. But those little packets also include a secret-weapon ingredient. Crumbled up, seaweed adds umami and richness to any dish. And when combined with soy sauce, you've got a potent combination that needs little else to shine. Pork chops (as long as they aren't oversized) are quick under a broiler, and as long as you slather them in yogurt, they won't dry out. Make sure not to overcook—contrary to popular opinion, pork can be a bit pink in the middle, just as with steak. So with a killer flavor combo on one of the easiest meats, you'll have a decadent dinner in no time.

Ingredients

4 tablespoons soy sauce

½ cup (125 g / 4 oz) Greek yogurt

1 teaspoon Kosher salt

8 grams roasted seaweed snacks (about 1 cup when crumbled)

4 pork chops

Make sure your top rack is only four inches from the top, and turn on your broiler. In a bowl, combine the soy sauce, yogurt, and salt. Crumble the seaweed snacks into pieces and stir half of them into the sauce. Slather the pork chops in the mixture. Place the chops on an aluminum-foil-lined tray and place under the broiler. Cook for four minutes on each side (if you want to check the temperature, it should be around 140 degrees Fahrenheit in the center). Sprinkle the remaining seaweed on top. Serve hot and pair with a side of rice or bread to round it out as a whole meal.

STUFFED CABBAGE *without the* STUFFING

No matter what else is on a menu, my husband will always order a stuffed cabbage if he sees it. There's something perfectly comforting about the silky heft of cabbage melding with the heartiness of meat and aided by the acidity of tomatoes. But you don't need a day of slow braising to get the same sensation. Cut the cabbage into pieces, use ground meat (I am partial to pork, but you can easily sub in beef), and add a zing with cider vinegar—you'll be all set for cold days in a matter of minutes.

Ingredients

2 tablespoons butter

2 small green cabbages

1 ½ teaspoons Kosher salt

4 cloves garlic

2 pounds (900 g / 32 oz) ground pork

⅓ (80 mL / 2.7 oz) cup apple cider vinegar

1 cup (200 g / 8 oz) crushed tomatoes

In a large Dutch oven or wok on medium high heat (but with more emphasis on the high), add the butter. Chop up the cabbage and add it to the pan, along with the salt. Stir occasionally, and let cook for three to four minutes until it starts to soften.

While the cabbage is cooking, chop the garlic. Throw it in and stir whenever you're done chopping.

Push the cabbage fully to the side of the pan and add the pork. Let it cook for three to four minutes, or until the pork browns on one side. Break up the pork with a spatula and add the cider vinegar and the tomatoes. Stir everything together and cook for another two to three minutes, or until the pork is just cooked through. Serve hot.

GORGONZOLA DOLCE, PEAR, *and* PROSCIUTTO WRAP

This is a four-ingredient meal that goes perfectly as a light lunch with a side of bread or as a lovely addition to a picnic. These little wraps are completely addictive once you get started. You can use this combination of flavors in so many other places too—use it on tartines, make a panini, throw it in pasta. There's something about the salty and sweet that no one can stop eating.

Ingredients

3 pears

1 head of lettuce for wraps (butter, Boston, or iceberg work well)

½ pound (225 g/8 oz) gorgonzola dolce

½ pound (225 g/8 oz) sliced prosciutto

Slice the pears. Place the pear slices on a piece of lettuce and add a spoonful of gorgonzola and then a slice of prosciutto on top. Wrap the lettuce together and repeat.

CHIMICHURRI STEAK *and* ZUCCHINI

My husband has family in Argentina, so I've always been a little biased in my love of chimichurri—but there truly are few combinations that brighten up a dish as effectively. The herbaceousness of the parsley and oregano gets a kick from the vinegar and garlic, and once you start making it, you'll find yourself throwing it on everything. I love pairing it with a flatiron steak—it's a more tender cut than skirt steak or hanger steak—but in a pinch, either of those would work well too.

Ingredients

Drizzle of a neutral oil like canola or vegetable

Heavy dash of Kosher salt, plus additional

2 pounds (900 g / 32 oz) flatiron steak (or skirt steak if you can't find flatiron), at room temperature

4 zucchini

1 large bunch fresh parsley

4 garlic cloves

2 tablespoons fresh oregano leaves (can sub 2 teaspoons dried oregano)

⅓ cup (80 mL / 2.7 oz) extra-virgin olive oil

3 tablespoons red wine vinegar

½ teaspoon red pepper flakes

Place a large grill pan, large griddle pan, or actual grill on high heat, brush it with oil, and let it heat up (if you don't have a large enough pan, you can always heat up two). Salt the steak generously on both sides. Cut the zucchini in half and then salt them as well.

When the pan is hot, place the steak and zucchini on it. Depending on your heat level, you'll want to cook both for three to four minutes on the first side—or until they have both browned deeply. Then turn the steak and zucchini over and cook for one to three minutes, depending on how rare you want your steak to be.

While the steak is cooking, make the chimichurri sauce. In a blender, add the parsley, garlic, oregano, olive oil, vinegar, red pepper flakes, and another dash of salt. Pulse so the sauce comes together but is still chunky.

When the steak and zucchini are done, remove them from the pan or grill and spread the chimichurri sauce on top.

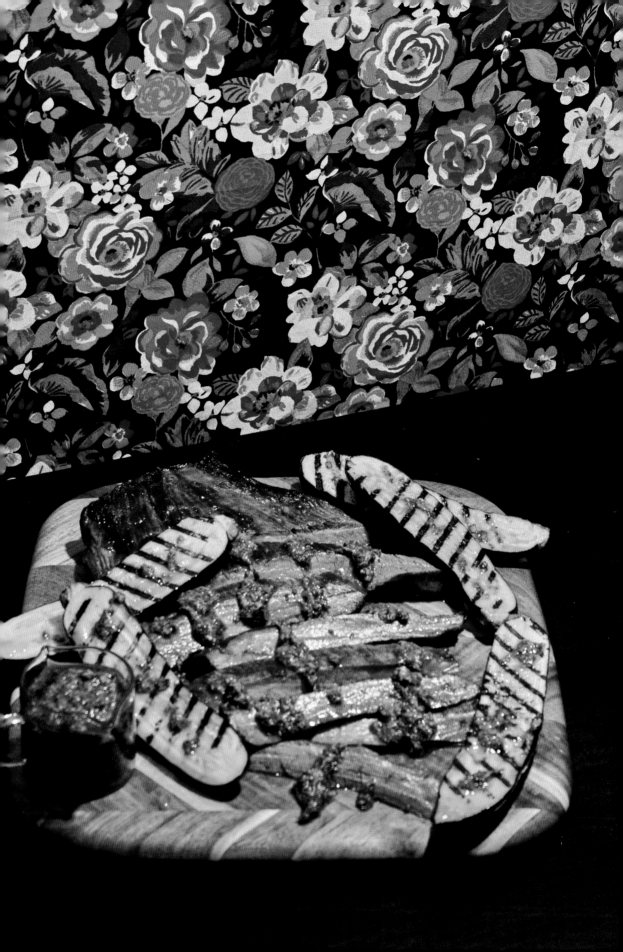

GINGER BEEF *and* BROCCOLI

The combination of beef and broccoli is classic for a reason—two satisfying ingredients meld perfectly together, making an entire meal. And this version uses two shortcuts whose quality has dramatically improved in recent years—beef strips and high-quality frozen vegetables can be game changers. Adding the blender (and skipping the arduous and unnecessary step of peeling) makes ginger quick, and the sauce will be one you keep going back to.

Ingredients

1 10-oz bag of frozen broccoli florets

2-inch knob of ginger (about 2 tablespoons—this makes for a very gingery dish, so level up or down as desired)

4 tablespoons soy sauce

1 tablespoon maple syrup

4 cloves garlic

6 scallions

2 pounds (900 g/32 oz) beef stir-fry strips

2 cups (250 g/16 oz) bean sprouts

1 teaspoon Kosher salt

Place a nonstick large skillet or wok on medium high heat. Add the broccoli to the wok and cook for three to four minutes or until the broccoli appears to have mostly defrosted (if you already have defrosted florets, you can skip this step and cook the broccoli with everything else).

While the broccoli is cooking, in a blender, combine the ginger, soy sauce, maple syrup, and garlic. Roughly chop the scallions.

Add the scallions, beef stir-fry strips, bean sprouts, and salt to the skillet with the broccoli. Let the stir fry cook without moving too much for two to three minutes—but be very careful, because the thinly cut beef will cook very quickly and can become chewy if cooked even a minute too long. Err on the side of a bit of pink in the beef.

When the beef is done cooking, remove from the heat immediately and pour the sauce on top. Combine and serve hot.

GROUND BEEF *with* KIMCHI TACOS

There are few items you could add to a dish to give it as much oomph as kimchi. It has spice, it has texture, it has flavor, it has umami. And in recent years we are seeing more and more smaller, higher-quality brands outside the mainstays. So seek it out. This dish thrives because the kimchi cuts through the meatiness of beef and goes perfectly with the crunch of tacos—but you could also use this beef and kimchi combo on everything from rice bowls to lettuce wraps to toast.

Ingredients

2 pounds (900 g/32 oz) of ground beef

Dash of Kosher salt

2 cups (224 g/8 oz) kimchi (napa cabbage versions preferred)

2 tablespoons rice vinegar

3 tablespoons soy sauce

6 scallions

2 Persian cucumbers (or half a small English cucumber)

8 to 12 taco shells or tortillas

Place a large nonstick sauté pan or wok on medium high heat and add the ground beef along with a dash of salt (you can drain some of the fat as it cooks if you need to).

Roughly chop the kimchi and then add that to the ground beef as well, along with the rice vinegar and soy sauce. Stir to combine. While the meat is cooking, chop the scallions, then add them to the wok.

While the beef continues cooking (typically around four to six minutes, depending on how high your heat is), slice the cucumbers as well.

When the beef has cooked (just barely lost its pink color), remove from the heat. Put the meat into the tacos and top with the cucumbers. Add another dash of salt. Taste to see if you need additional hot sauce, depending on the spiciness of your kimchi.

BEEF *and* CHICKPEAS *with* AQUAFABA

One of the coolest discoveries you can make is that the liquid chickpeas sit in can be whipped into a beautiful savory whipped-cream-like substance called aquafaba. It's so fast, yet it feels so fancy—and the bonus is, it can be like the flavorful topping giving creaminess to an otherwise meaty dish. I love this iteration because it is packed with flavor and especially fun for kids. If you want to skip the aquafaba, that's okay too—replace with a dollop of sour cream and you'll get a similar creaminess in the mix.

Ingredients

2 pounds (900 g/32 oz) ground beef

2 teaspoons chili powder

2 teaspoons garlic powder

2 teaspoons Kosher salt, plus additional

2 28-oz (794 g) cans cooked chickpeas

2 tablespoons mint

1 lemon

Place a large skillet on medium high heat. Add the beef, chili powder, garlic powder, and salt and cook for two to three minutes or until the meat begins to brown and you can break it into small pieces.

While the meat is cooking, drain a can of the chickpea liquid into your stand mixer with the whisk setting (you can also use a handheld beater). Turn it on and let it beat for three to five minutes, until it has the consistency of whipped cream and shows stiff peaks (if after that it hasn't started whipping up enough, you can add a pinch of cream of tartar). This is your aquafaba.

While the chickpea liquid is turning into aquafaba, drain the other can, and then add both cans of chickpeas to the meat mixture. Let it all cook another three to four minutes.

While the chickpea mixture is cooking, chop the mint. Put the mint and the juice of the lemon into the aquafaba and mix it in.

When the meat is done, stir in about half the aquafaba mixture. Serve hot and top with the remaining aquafaba (it melts, so do it only right before serving).

HOISIN BEEF WRAP

Even if you haven't ever used hoisin at home, you are undoubtedly familiar with the sweet and savory flavor of this sauce that you find in everything from Peking duck to pho. It's one of those essential condiments—once you start using it, you'll put it on everything. It can be a dip, it can be a marinade, it can be a finishing sauce. But in this recipe, it is paired with pickled ginger to give tons of flavor to simple beef lettuce wraps. Something this easy shouldn't taste this good, but that's the magic of hoisin.

Ingredients

Dash of olive oil

2 pounds (900 g / 32 oz) ground beef (lean preferred)

4 tablespoons hoisin sauce

4 tablespoons pickled ginger

1 cup (125 g / 4.5 oz) peanuts

4 scallions

1 head of lettuce for wraps (butter, Boston, or iceberg work well)

Place a pan on medium high heat with olive oil. Add the ground beef with the hoisin sauce. Chop the ginger and add that too. Cook for five minutes or until the beef has just stopped being pink (you don't want to overcook). If your beef has an excess of oil, you can drain it.

While the beef is cooking, chop the peanuts and the scallions roughly. When the beef is done, remove from the heat, add the peanuts and scallions, and mix together. Add the beef mixture to each piece of lettuce and wrap together to serve.

GREEN OLIVE *and* ROSEMARY LAMB CHOPS

This dish is such a banger that it has become my go-to for when I have guests coming over and want them to feel like I went all-out, but actually don't want to spend more than fifteen minutes making anything. Lamb chops feel decadent, but under the broiler they become a quick treat. And bulgur—which we normally reserve only for tabbouleh for some reason—cooks in ten minutes and is a superstar at melding the flavors of the olive and rosemary. A one-stop shop from start to finish! Just a note, the timing here will cook your chops to medium rare. If you want to cook them more, you certainly can, but I recommend eating them with a pink center (and that's also how you can keep this to fifteen minutes).

Ingredients

1 cup bulgur (medium or fine grain if you want it to not take too long)

1 lemon

2 teaspoons Kosher salt

1 cup (180 g/6 oz) green olives, Castelvetrano preferred

2 tablespoons rosemary

¼ cup mayonnaise

8 lamb chops

4 Persian (or small seedless) cucumbers

Bring two cups of water to a boil. Place an oven rack close to your burner. Turn on your oven's broiler. Line a sheet tray with aluminum foil. Add the bulgur to the water (whether it's boiling or not) along with the juice of the lemon and one teaspoon of salt. Cover the pot. When it starts to boil, turn it down to a simmer.

Chop the olives and the rosemary until both are fairly small. Take roughly two-thirds of the olives and about half the rosemary and add them to the bulgur.

In a bowl, combine the rest of the rosemary and olives, the mayonnaise, and the remaining salt. Spread the mixture across both sides of the lamb chops and place them on the sheet tray. Put the chops in the oven under the broiler for three to four minutes, and then flip the chops to the other side. Cook for an additional three to four minutes.

While the chops and bulgur are cooking, smash the cucumbers with the back of a knife, and then roughly chop them. When you are a minute out from getting the lamb chops, fold the cucumbers in with the bulgur. Serve everything hot.

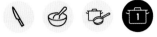

LAMB *and* SMASHED CUCUMBER STUFFED PITAS

This recipe is all about texture—from the silkiness of the tahini to the craggy crunch of the smashed cucumbers. The pita allows for everything to merge together at once, creating a symphony of flavors packed into one delicious pouch. You can heat up your pitas for ten seconds in the microwave if you want everything to be warm, but one thing I love about this dish is that it can work at any temperature. If you don't have pomegranate molasses (although you should get it!), you can sub in pomegranate seeds or lemon to get that bright acidity. You can serve this with a tzatziki or yogurt lemon sauce to dip it in if you want some extra flavor.

Ingredients

2 pounds (900 g / 32 oz) ground lamb

1 teaspoon cinnamon

2 teaspoons cumin

2 teaspoons Kosher salt

2 tablespoons pomegranate molasses

½ cup tahini

4 Persian cucumbers (or other small cucumber)

4 pitas

Parsley for garnish

In a sauté pan on medium high heat, add the lamb and half the cinnamon, cumin, and salt. Cook for five to seven minutes, or until the lamb is just cooked through.

While the lamb is cooking, add the remaining cinnamon, cumin, and salt to a bowl and add the pomegranate molasses and tahini. Whisk together. Using the side of a knife (or bottom of a frying pan), smash the cucumbers and then roughly chop them so they are bite-size. Add the cucumbers to the tahini mixture and combine.

When the lamb is done cooking, drain the excess fat and toss the lamb with the cucumber mixture. Add the lamb and cucumbers to a pita and top with some parsley to garnish.

08

VEGGIE
MEALS

SPICY TOMATO SHAKSHUKA

If I see shakshuka on a menu I almost always order it—it's like a Pavlovian response. There's something about tomatoes and eggs that is irresistible. But it's incredibly easy to make at home too—and this version eschews anything that takes time, like chopping onions or peppers. However, that doesn't mean it lacks flavor. I love using harissa, a spicy condiment from North Africa that is now more widely available. It adds a ton of complexity and spice without any work. Throw in some olives along with roasted red peppers, and you have a burst of flavor without a lot of time spent.

Ingredients

2 28-oz (794 g) cans diced tomatoes

1 teaspoon Kosher salt, plus additional

⅓ cup (60 g/2 oz) pitted kalamata olives

1 cup (150 g/5 oz) roasted red peppers

2 teaspoons cumin

2 teaspoons harissa

Large bunch of parsley

6 large eggs

Place a large saucepan or Dutch oven on medium high heat. Add the diced tomatoes, salt, olives, red peppers, cumin, and harissa and stir together. Bring the mixture up to a heavy simmer. Tear apart the parsley (or roughly chop if you'd rather), then add that in. Create little wells for the eggs. Crack the eggs into the pan, add another dash of salt on top, and then cover for six to eight minutes, or until the whites have set but the yolk is still runny. Serve hot.

LENTIL SKILLET *with* RICOTTA, CORN, *and* AVOCADO

One of my all-time favorite recipes is Ellie Krieger's lentil skillet. Before Ellie taught me, I'd never really thought to use canned lentils, and now they are one of my ultimate staples. This recipe puts a twist on her version by adding a bit more spice to the proceedings and bringing in the complementary flavors of corn and avocado. But swap this one around as much as you like—the base idea of lentils and ricotta pairs so well with whatever you have in your fridge that you'll find yourself coming back to this combo again and again, like me.

Ingredients

2 15-oz (400 g) cans of cooked lentils

1 teaspoon salt, plus additional

2 oz (30 g) spinach

1 teaspoon chili powder

½ teaspoon ground cumin

1 teaspoon garlic powder

1 jar (340 g/12 oz) roasted red peppers

1 cup (225 g/8 oz) frozen corn

Small bunch of cilantro

1 avocado

1 cup (225 g/8 oz) ricotta

Heat a large skillet over medium heat. Drain the lentils and then add them, salt, spinach, chili powder, cumin, and garlic powder to the skillet. Stir to combine. Drain the red peppers, then add them and the corn into the lentil mixture. Cover and cook, stirring occasionally, for four to five minutes.

While the lentils are cooking, roughly chop the cilantro and dice the avocado.

Make a few wells in the lentil mixture and dollop spoonfuls of the ricotta into it. Add the avocado on top and sprinkle more salt. Cover and cook for another minute, and then spread the cilantro on top. Serve hot.

GREEN SHAKSHUKA

This one-pot meal is as satisfying as it is easy. Practically everything comes out of a can, yet it tastes as fresh and bright as possible because of the combination of salsa verde and feta. Do make sure to seek out a good salsa verde, though—this recipe is only as good as the ingredients you start with.

Ingredients

2 14-oz (400 g) cans of quartered artichokes

Heavy drizzle of extra-virgin olive oil

10 oz (282 g) previously frozen spinach

Dash of Kosher salt

4 cups (900 g/32 oz) salsa verde

2 teaspoons garlic powder

Small bunch of cilantro (or 1 tablespoon ground coriander)

8 eggs

2 avocados

8 oz (227 g) feta

Place a large pan or Dutch oven on medium high heat. Drain the artichokes. Add the olive oil, spinach, artichokes, and dash of salt to the pan and cook down for one minute.

Add the salsa verde and garlic powder and bring up to a heavy simmer.

Lightly chop the cilantro, then stir it in. Create little wells for the eggs. Crack the eggs into the pan, add another dash of salt on top, and then cover for six to eight minutes, or until the whites have almost set but the yolk is still runny.

While the eggs are cooking, cut the avocado into small pieces and crumble the feta. Add to the pan and cover for one more minute. Serve hot.

OMELETTE PIZZA

This is one of those dishes that somehow feels like pure fun and yet is surprisingly healthy. The eggs take the place of pizza dough (which, I know, will probably cause a few people to scoff at calling this pizza in any way, but just go with it). The tomato sauce, basil, and mozzarella combo goes perfectly. As with all pizzas, feel free to go wild with whatever toppings strike your fancy. It's that perfect "breakfast for any meal" kind of dish that everyone will be a fan of.

Ingredients

Drizzle of olive oil

10 eggs

½ teaspoon Kosher salt, plus additional

¼ (60 mL/2 oz) cup milk

1 cup (250 mL/8 oz) tomato sauce

1 ball mozzarella

Small bunch basil

Place a very wide pan (preferably nonstick) on medium heat with enough olive oil to coat the bottom. Crack the eggs into a bowl and add the salt and milk. Whisk together. Pour the eggs into the pan, cover, and let cook for six to eight minutes, until almost fully cooked. Every two minutes or so you want to check in by lifting and tilting the eggs, i.e., use a spatula to lift up the edge of the omelette and tilt the pan to allow the runny eggs to fill in the space. It will make the omelette cook faster and more evenly.

Measure out the tomato sauce and chop the mozzarella. Lightly tear the basil (or don't, if it's small). Add the tomato sauce, then the mozzarella, then the basil, on top of the eggs. Sprinkle more salt on top, then cover. Cook another minute or two until the mozzarella has begun to melt. Cut into slices and serve hot.

SPAGHETTI SQUASH POMODORO

This recipe almost verges on ridiculous—you cut a giant vegetable in half, stick it in a microwave, and then pour some sauce on it? That's it? But seriously—that's it. It's delightful. It makes you feel ingenious. And it'll get anyone in your household excited about vegetables. It's also a great receptacle for leftovers and riffs. What more could you ask for?

Ingredients

2 small to medium-sized spaghetti squash

Dash of Kosher salt

Small bunch basil

2 cups (500 mL / 16 oz) marinara sauce

Grated parmesan cheese

Using a very sharp knife, carefully cut the spaghetti squash in half. Scoop out the seeds and add water into the center of each until it's almost "full." Place the squash in a microwave (you can do this in a dish or, if you're especially lazy like me, you can just place them on your microwave's turntable). Cook for eight to ten minutes (or less if your squash are small). While the squash is cooking, chop your basil. Combine the basil, marinara sauce, and cheese (to your taste).

When the squash is done, remove it from the microwave and dump out the water. Scrape the interior a bit to get the "spaghetti" texture, but leave everything in the squash—it will act as its own bowl. Pour the sauce on top. Eat hot.

SAVORY FRENCH TOAST

Who doesn't want French toast for dinner? This savory version is the perfect quick companion for a night in—it feels like a delightful play on a classic, yet you'll feel as sated as though you'd had a bowl of creamy pasta.

Ingredients

2 tablespoons canola oil

2 tablespoons butter (or more as needed)

4 eggs

½ cup (125 mL/4 oz) sour cream (at room temperature if possible)

½ cup (45 g) grated parmesan

1 teaspoon Kosher salt

1 teaspoon garlic powder

Dash of fresh pepper

8 to 10 slices bread (brioche, challah, or other thick, soft bread preferred)

Handful of herbs like parsley, cilantro, or basil

Put a griddle pan (or two large pans) on medium high heat. Add half the oil and butter to the pan.

In a bowl, whisk the eggs and sour cream together. Add the parmesan, salt, garlic powder, and pepper, then combine.

Dip two slices (or more, depending on your pan size) in the egg mixture and place on the pan. Let cook for two to four minutes, until the bread has browned, and flip, cooking the same amount on the other side. Add more butter and oil as needed, and dip and cook all the bread.

Chop the herbs as desired and sprinkle on top (but only if you want to—you don't need them to have a complete dish).

SHEET PAN ASPARAGUS *and* EGGS

Asparagus and eggs make the simplest light breakfast or lunch meal. While we might not usually think to broil our eggs, I actually love the silky poached texture that makes a perfect contrast to the asparagus. And most importantly, it's a one-pan, minimal-cleanup healthy option.

Ingredients

1 pound (454 g) asparagus

2 tablespoons fresh oregano

Heavy dash of olive oil and salt

1 lemon

4 room-temperature eggs

½ cup (30 g) panko crumbs

Grated parmesan

Place an oven rack four to six inches from your broiler (err on the closer side if your broiler isn't that strong). Turn the broiler on. Line a sheet pan with aluminum foil.

Place the asparagus on the sheet tray and toss them in the oregano, olive oil, and salt, and the juice of the lemon. Make sure you've tossed enough that the foil is covered in oil as well.

Making space for the eggs, crack the eggs into the middle of the pan, surrounded by the asparagus. Top with more oil and salt. Place the sheet pan in the oven. Cook for three or four minutes, or until the egg whites have begun to set and the asparagus is beginning to char. Make sure to watch because broiling is very oven-dependent, so some eggs will cook even faster.

Remove from the oven and add the panko crumbs on top. Cook for another minute or until the panko has browned. Top with the parmesan and eat hot.

GORGONZOLA *and* RADICCHIO *with* WHITE BEANS *and* SPINACH

I've always been a little obsessed with the combination of gorgonzola and radicchio. You see this salty, bitter, creamy duo across Italy, but for some reason rarely elsewhere. Maybe it's polarizing, but sometimes polarizing just means a wallop of flavor. And with barely any work, you have a hefty greens and beans meal that won't feel like you're merely settling for something healthy.

Ingredients

Dash of olive oil

1 small head radicchio

6 cups (250 g) spinach

2 15-oz (400 g) cans cannellini beans

Dash of Kosher salt

Dash of pepper

1 lemon

¼ pound (113 g/4 oz) crumbled gorgonzola

Place a large saucepan or wok on high heat and add the olive oil. Chop the radicchio into bite-sized pieces. Add the radicchio and half the spinach to the pan and cook for three to four minutes, or until the radicchio begins to wilt.

Drain the cans of beans, then add them, along with the remaining spinach and a dash of salt and pepper, to the radicchio and spinach mixture. Juice the lemon into the pan as well. Cook for another two minutes. Add the gorgonzola to the pan and remove from the heat. Let the cheese melt, taste, and add salt and pepper as needed (depending on the saltiness of your beans and gorgonzola, you might need a varying amount). Serve hot.

GREEK SALAD TACOS

I constantly feel lucky to live in a golden age of ingredients and influences—none of which is more apparent than the simple perfection of putting classic Greek salad ingredients inside the crunch of a taco. It's not traditional to anyone, but it sure is a delicious way to have an easy, no-cook meal.

Ingredients

1 cup (180 g/6 oz) pitted kalamata olives

¼ cup (60 mL/2 oz) Greek yogurt

6 Persian cucumbers (or 1 large English cucumber)

1 red bell pepper

1½ cups (350 g/12 oz) cherry tomatoes

Small bunch mint leaves

1 lemon

Dash of Kosher salt

8 to 12 taco shells or tortillas

4 oz (113 g) feta cheese

Put the kalamata olives and Greek yogurt in a large bowl. Then prep the rest of your ingredients—dice the cucumbers, pepper, and cherry tomatoes (these can be fairly large, don't spend too much time). Chop up the mint. Add all the chopped ingredients to the bowl, then juice the lemon on top. Add a dash of salt and combine. Place the salad mixture into the taco shells or tortillas and top with crumbled feta cheese.

VEGGIE SLOPPY JOE

I don't think anything makes kids much happier than the gooey mess of a sloppy joe. But you don't always have to include meat in the equation! This recipe uses lentils and mushrooms to get that perfect blend, along with a simple but effective sloppy joe sauce. When you want something easy and crowd-pleasing, it's hard to go wrong with this!

Ingredients

1 15-oz (400 g) can of cooked lentils

1 pound (454 g) portobello mushrooms

½ cup (125 mL/4 oz) tomato sauce

1 tablespoon tomato paste

2 tablespoons Worcestershire sauce

1 tablespoon maple syrup

½ tablespoon white vinegar

Dash of Kosher salt

Dash of pepper

4 burger buns

Drain the can of lentils. Put the mushrooms in your food processor or blender (or, if you really want to chop it up, go right ahead—just make sure it's pretty finely chopped). Place the mushrooms in a large saucepan along with the lentils, tomato sauce, tomato paste, Worcestershire sauce, maple syrup, white vinegar, and a generous dash of salt and pepper. Bring the heat up to medium high and let the mixture come to a simmer. Cook for five minutes or until the mushrooms have softened. Taste to see if any additional salt is needed.

Put the mixture on the burger buns and eat hot.

SMASHED PEA TOAST *with* SESAME *and* CHILI

Step aside, avocado toast, and get ready to love the smashed pea toast! Unlike finicky avocado (which can go from unripe to brown in what feels like a matter of minutes), this toast is almost entirely a pantry creation that has the bonus of being a no-cook wonder.

Ingredients

1 lemon

1 pound (454 g/16 oz) green peas (if previously frozen, make sure they are defrosted)

2 tablespoons sesame oil

2 teaspoons chili powder

Salt to taste

4 tablespoons sesame seeds

½ cup (113 g/4 oz) ricotta

4 to 8 slices of bread (toasted or untoasted)

Juice the lemon into a bowl. Add in the peas, sesame oil, and chili powder. Using the back of a spoon or potato masher, mash the peas roughly. You don't want the mixture to be smooth—it should be still rather chunky. Add the salt and most of the sesame seeds and combine again. Taste to make sure there's enough salt.

Spread the ricotta lightly across the toast and then place the pea mixture on top. Sprinkle the remaining sesame seeds on top.

MUSHROOM RICOTTA TOAST

This toast is so simple and yet so delectable. There's something about the meaty umami of mushrooms brightened with a bit of sherry vinegar on top of creamy savory ricotta. And bread makes everything better. So if you see some particularly great mushrooms at the store or market, keep it simple with this easy meal.

Ingredients

2 pints (300 g) variety of wild mushrooms (I love a mix of cremini, oyster, Lion's Mane, beech, maitake, and/or royal trumpet, but anything you like works here)

4 garlic cloves

¼ cup (60 mL/2 oz) olive oil

¼ (60 mL/2 oz) cup sherry vinegar

Dash of Kosher salt

1 cup (225 g/8 oz) ricotta

4 large slices rustic bread

Place a pan on medium heat with the olive oil in it. Chop the wild mushrooms into bite-sized pieces and slice the garlic. Toss the mushrooms and garlic into the pan. Cook for three to five minutes, or until the mushrooms have softened. Remove from the heat and toss in the sherry vinegar and salt. Spread the ricotta onto the slices of bread and add another dash of salt. Top the bread with the mushroom and garlic mixture. Serve hot.

GOAT CHEESE *and* OLIVE ENGLISH MUFFIN PIZZAS

Classic English muffin pizzas might be my husband's all-time favorite thing to eat. It's his go-to thing to make, and it always makes a crowd happy. While you certainly *can* make the classic Margherita style, I wanted a bit of a twist—and you can make your own versions too, swapping out cheeses and toppings to your heart's content! Use the base and make pizzas your own way every time, without the mess of dough.

Ingredients

4 English muffins

1 cup (250 mL/8 oz) marinara

Handful of spinach

4 oz (113 g) of soft goat cheese

Handful of pitted kalamata olives (or whichever olives you prefer)

Dash of Kosher salt

Fresh basil for garnish

Preheat your broiler (this recipe is much easier in a toaster oven, but a regular oven is fine too). You want to make sure the rack is fairly close to the top.

Line a sheet tray with aluminum foil. Halve the English muffins and place them, craggy side up, on the sheet tray. Spread around a tablespoon of marinara on each muffin. Add some spinach leaves on top. Then add the goat cheese in dollops, followed by the olives. Add a dash of salt.

Place the sheet tray in the oven under the broiler for two to four minutes or until the cheese is melted and everything is bubbling a bit. Remove from the oven and top with a few basil leaves. Serve hot.

HUMMUS QUESADILLA *with* SPINACH *and* ARTICHOKE

I love a good quesadilla stuffed with cheese, but sometimes you need to liven things up (and maybe even try and make them a little more of a full balanced meal). With hummus, you get all the creaminess of cheese, but with a new flavor combination. This is a simple weeknight meal that is as easy as it gets.

Ingredients

Drizzle of olive oil

1 14-oz (400 g) can of quartered artichoke hearts

8 tortillas

1 cup (250 g) hummus

Large handful of spinach

Dash of Kosher salt

Warm a large skillet on medium heat and brush on a very light coating of olive oil. Lightly chop the artichoke hearts. On the first two or three tortillas, spread the hummus evenly. Cover half of each tortilla, moderately, with some spinach, artichoke hearts, and a dash of salt. Fold the uncovered half on top to make a half-moon shape.

Place two or three quesadillas in the pan (depending on how many fit—you don't want to overcrowd). While the quesadillas are cooking, prep the remaining tortillas. Let the quesadillas cook for two to three minutes, or until the bottom is golden brown, and then flip. Let cook for another two to three minutes. Remove from the pan and then continue with the remaining quesadillas. Serve hot.

TOFU KUNG PAO-ISH

Kung Pao is one of those favorites we often only eat at a restaurant or for takeout—the traditional Sichuan dish has a storied history, and as home cooks, we may not have easy access to ingredients like Sichuan peppercorns or black vinegar. But as chili oil and chili crisp have become mainstays of our grocery stores, the opportunity to make a version at home is more possible. So this is -ish because it's certainly just an homage—but one that I think gets toward that tingly, spicy, sweet, and vinegary combination. If you can't find chili oil or chili crisp (do look online first), you can always sub in sesame oil with a chili paste, or even chili flakes. But try to seek it out, because it's one of those products we are so lucky to have more in abundance now, and that peppercorn flavor is truly unique.

Ingredients

2 teaspoons vegetable oil

14 oz (400 g) extra firm tofu

3 cloves garlic

1 bunch of scallions

1 tablespoon corn starch

3 tablespoons soy sauce

2 tablespoons rice wine vinegar (or balsamic if you don't have rice wine)

2 tablespoons brown sugar

2 tablespoons chili crisp or chili oil

Dash of Kosher salt

1/3 cup (42 g / 1.5 oz) whole roasted peanuts

16 oz (454 g) shredded carrots

16 oz (454 g) frozen green beans

16 oz (454 g) snow peas

Place a large wok or saucepan on high heat with the vegetable oil. Cut the tofu into one-inch cubes. Add the tofu to the pan and cook for five minutes or until it has browned, stirring occasionally.

While the tofu is cooking, mince the garlic and chop the scallions. In a small bowl, combine the corn starch, soy sauce, vinegar, brown sugar, and chili crisp/oil.

Remove the tofu from the pan, sprinkle a bit of salt on it, and set it aside. Add the garlic, scallions, peanuts, carrots, green beans, and snow peas to the pan, along with the sauce. Cook for approximately two minutes, or until everything has softened a bit. Add the tofu back in. Gently stir it all together and then add any additional salt as needed. Serve hot.

SEAWEEDY SOY COLLARDS
and WHITE BEANS

I love any recipe combo of greens and beans because they make for the easiest balanced meal. This one has extra oomph from the seaweed, which gives a depth to the collard and white bean combo. You can eat this on its own or mix and match as you'd like—it goes great on toast or on top of rice.

Ingredients

⅓ cup (80 mL/2.7 oz) soy sauce

⅓ cup (80 mL/2.7 oz) sesame oil

2 large bunches of collard greens

12 oz (around 1 ½ cups when crumbled) roasted seaweed

3 15-oz (400 g) cans cannellini beans

Dash of Kosher salt

In a large wok or saucepan on high heat, add the soy sauce and sesame oil. Chop the collard greens. Add them to the wok. Chop or rip the seaweed into small pieces. Add to the wok and combine with the collards. Cook for at least five minutes, or until the collards have wilted.

While the collards are cooking, drain the beans. Add the beans to the wok and combine. Taste to see if any additional salt is needed—because the seaweed, beans, and soy sauce can often have a lot of salt, you may not need much (or any). Serve hot.

09

BONUS! DESSERTS

KEY LIME SANDWICH COOKIE

I love key lime pie, but sometimes you just need a quicker route to a flavor. These little sandwich cookies are addictive heaven—you get all the creamy tartness of key lime filling, but with so much less work. And don't worry if you can't find key limes. You can use regular limes if you want, but just keep in mind you might only need one or two, since key limes are so much smaller. Just make sure you are using fresh juice, because the lime flavor is what makes this recipe sing.

Ingredients

3 key limes (or about 2 tablespoons fresh key lime juice)

4 oz (110 g) cream cheese

⅓ cup (45 g) powdered sugar

¼ teaspoon Kosher salt

20 tea biscuits (Maria cookies work best, but digestives, ginger snaps, or even halved graham crackers work well)

Juice the limes into a bowl and add the cream cheese, sugar, and salt. Mix fully (you can use a hand beater or a stand mixer or even your own two hands—just make sure everything is whipped together completely).

Place a generous dollop on one side of a cookie and then put another cookie on top. Repeat until you have made as many sandwich cookies as you can with the filling.

S'MORES ICE CREAM SANDWICH

Everyone loves a s'more—but why not add another beloved item and throw ice cream into the mix? We think of the classic dessert as a summertime delight, but with your toaster oven you can have it year-round. So skip the campfire and have a treat in just a few minutes at home!

Ingredients

8 marshmallows

8 graham crackers

Chocolate ice cream

Turn on the broiler setting of your toaster oven—you can do this in a regular oven too, if you don't have a toaster oven. Line a sheet tray with aluminum foil and place the marshmallows on top. Cook for thirty seconds to a minute on each side, or until they char, turning once they start to char, but before they burn.

While the marshmallows are cooking, break the graham crackers in half. Scoop a small scoop of ice cream onto eight of the graham cracker halves. Remove the marshmallows from the oven. Scoop them on top of the ice cream and then place the remaining graham crackers on top. Eat immediately.

BRÛLÉED GRAPEFRUIT

This is one of those casual desserts that has a fancy name but feels so simple to make that it almost can't be classified as a recipe. There's no measuring needed because the simplicity and ease are what makes it work. But it's the perfect sweet light treat for a weekday. Or you can even prep it ahead and then just stick it under the broiler for guests after a heavy meal. It's a treat without the work—just make sure you have a good broiler, because this recipe really doesn't work without it.

Ingredients

2 large red grapefruits

Brown sugar

Cinnamon

Honey

Flaky sea salt

Place your oven rack as close to the top as it will go. Turn on your broiler. Line a sheet tray with aluminum foil. Cut the grapefruits in half and, using a sharp (or serrated, in a pinch) knife, cut around the perimeter to free the fruit from the peel, and then cut in between the segments. This doesn't need to be exact—it's just to help free up the segments for eating later, but you can certainly serve this with a knife so that the rest of the work can be done while eating.

Place the grapefruits on the sheet tray, flesh side up. Sprinkle a healthy dose of brown sugar and cinnamon on top and then drizzle on honey. Finish with the flaky sea salt. Put under the broiler for around five minutes, or until the grapefruit has started to caramelize but not yet burn.

SALTED CHOCOLATE PUDDING

We think of pudding as taking a long time, but as long as you like it warm (which I think enhances it), you can make this very quickly with only a few ingredients that you probably already have lying around. But if you want to cool it down, it's also a great one to make ahead and store in the fridge for later.

Ingredients

½ cup (100 g) sugar

3 tablespoons cocoa powder

⅓ cup (58 g/2 oz) dark chocolate chips (I like at least 80 percent)

¼ teaspoon flaky sea salt, plus additional

3 tablespoons cornstarch

2 cups (500 mL/16 oz) milk

In a medium saucepan, combine the sugar, cocoa powder, chocolate chips, salt, and cornstarch with a whisk. Add the milk, turn on the heat to medium and whisk. Stir occasionally, but once it starts to simmer and it thickens, you'll want to stir more—be careful not to over-stir, it doesn't need a ton of whisking, but you just want to move it around as it heats. From the point of simmer, it should only take one to two minutes to thicken and resemble pudding. Remove from the heat.

You can serve it hot or chilled. Top with a lot of flaky sea salt and any other toppings you want—nuts, berries, more chocolate, and whipped cream all go great.

CHOCOLATE RASPBERRY MOUSSE

What could possibly be better than chocolate mousse? How about chocolate mousse with the tart sweetness of raspberries folded in? The bonus here is that, because of the raspberries, you don't need any sugar, and this becomes one of those perfect four ingredient-wonders that will have everyone asking for the recipe.

Ingredients

1 cup (125 g) raspberries, plus additional

¾ cup (130 g / 4.5 oz) dark chocolate chips

1 ½ (375 mL / 12 oz) cups cold heavy cream

¼ cup (30 g) unsweetened cocoa powder

To a microwave-safe bowl, add the raspberries and chocolate chips. Place in the microwave for thirty seconds. Remove and stir, smushing the raspberries into the chocolate. Microwave for fifteen more seconds, then stir again. If the chocolate hasn't melted, repeat.

In a mixer, beat the heavy cream until it turns into whipped cream (at least a minute, sometimes taking up for four or five minutes depending on your cream or mixer). You want the whipped cream to hold firm but not be over-whipped—it should look like firm peaks, where if you take the whisk out of the bowl, the whipped cream holds up, but still is a little soft (if you're unsure what it should look like, do an image search on firm peaks and you'll see it).

When the whipped cream is ready, add the cocoa powder to the bowl and fold it in with a flexible spatula. Then add the melted chocolate mixture. You can fold it in with the whisk on a low speed. When everything has fully combined, the mousse is ready.

You can serve as is, or place in the fridge for later. Top with another raspberry to serve.

WHIPPED CREAM *and* STRAWBERRIES

I feel like a broken record when it comes to extolling the virtues and ease of making homemade whipped cream—because that's really all it entails, just whipping up some cream. This is, again, one of those recipes that doesn't really seem like a recipe but that's the beauty of it: because you made the whipped cream—and because everyone loves the combination of strawberries and whipped cream—you literally don't need to do anything other than put out a bowl of whipped cream and strawberries to have a fantastic quick dessert. You certainly can cut the strawberries if you want, but I find people are just as happy using their hands to pick up a strawberry and dipping it in the cream. So why waste the time? Just enjoy the simple perfection of strawberries and cream. Try to buy the best-quality ingredients you can, since this is so simple.

Ingredients

1 cup (250 mL / 8 oz) heavy whipping cream (a high-quality organic version if you can)

1 pound (450 g) organic strawberries

Using a mixer or hand blender (or by hand with a whisk if you have the stamina), whip the cream until it has the texture of whipped cream. The timing will completely depend on what instrument you use, but just watch it carefully to make sure the cream is stiff and holds peaks, but is not over-whipped.

Place the whipped cream and the strawberries in separate bowls and serve as is—yes, you really don't have to do anything else, and people will dip it in just fine!

ACKNOWLEDGMENTS

I feel so incredibly lucky to be publishing my third cookbook. To get the opportunity to be in people's homes and (hopefully) make their lives easier is the greatest gift I could have ever asked for. So the first and foremost thanks is to *you*, for trusting me with your time, your wallet, and your palate.

I am so grateful to Mango Publishing for being the one and only place where I wanted this book to live. I'm completely inspired by what you guys are accomplishing, simply by being willing to examine tradition and upend what needs to be upended. Thank you for letting me join your mission. Brenda Knight, we hit it off right from the word go, and I feel so lucky to be shepherded in your capable hands. To the rest of Team Mango—especially Chris McKenney, Elina Diaz, Geena El-Haj, Hannah Jorstad Paulsen, Lisa McGuinness, Christina Hodgkinson, Minerve Jean, Nehemie Pierre, Robin Miller, and Veronica Diaz—thank you for the incredible work you do. Your support for this book and all your authors has been marvelous to see. And on that note: Thank you so much to Alison Fargis for finding this book its proper home. You listened to all my gripes about the strange state of publishing and immediately said, "I know the solution." I'm so appreciative of you.

The photos in this book are truly more beautiful than they have any right to be. This is a book about making food amidst the backdrop of messy glorious real life and I wanted that to always feel like it had the potential to be *fun* rather than a daily slog. Noah Fecks, Ethan Lunkenheimer, and Ashton Keefe were—once again—the ultimate dream team. Noah, your photos have life and vibrancy in a way no one else seems to capture. But, more importantly, you are the kindest soul who gives so much of yourself to others. I'm incredibly lucky to call you a friend; thank you for being in my corner. Ethan, I could watch you spin magic out of disparate props forever. Your eye is unmatched. Thank you for sharing your talents with this book and making everything infinitely more fun, both in real life and in photos. Ashton, if we weren't such good friends outside of work, I would genuinely believe you were a robot. No one else is as precise and methodical while also somehow having innate creative instincts. I'll never get over watching you turn from my bubbly confidante into a cooking and styling machine. Thank you for somehow agreeing to be my wing woman when I need you. I will always be yours (though not in styling, because, let's face it, you wouldn't want me there, ha ha).

It's always been extremely important to me to have my recipes tested outside my kitchen by the kind of home cooks I hope will use this book. But to make that happen, dozens of people have to volunteer to cook and give honest feedback. To all the *15 Minute Meal* recipe testers: thank you so much for taking the time to make this book the best it could be. Having your perspectives and getting to see how each recipe stood up in another kitchen was imperative. This book is indebted to you. Thank you, Amy Rogers,

Ariel Kantor, Alana Rush, Carla Siegel, Carly Goldsmith, Deepika Misra Jones, Emily Vickers, Gracie Swansburg, Hilary Vandam, Jane Bruce, Jessica Chou, Erin Zumbrun, Josh Zumbrun, Juliet Izon, Katie Reisert, Kristina Conner, Lauren Shockey, Lisa Micich, Liz Slade, Melissa Jerves, Patricia Lloyd, Sarah Covey, Sarah Strong, Sophie Doering, Stephanie Philips, Susan Corning, and Tiffany Peón. And thank you to friends and family who tasted recipes as I made them and gave honest feedback, including Miriam, Gabe, Rudy, Celina, Chris, Alex, and Lauren. Thank you also so much to the other cookbook authors who let me vent and bounce ideas, especially Yasmin Fahr and Charlotte Druckman. And to Jeannie Chen for assisting so beautifully when we needed a pinch hitter!

People ask me a lot how I "get it all done" and the honest answer is I have a lot of help. Childcare professionals make working mothers possible, and we should shout from the rooftops about our gratitude for them. Ellie Bernal and Lucy Fernandes, you both truly made this book possible, so thank you.

My family is my best support. I love all my Gourbralters—Yehuda, Natalie, Aaron, Leo, and Rachel. To Annie, Will, Skye, and Jon (and my niece and nephew who will be here by the time this book arrives and I already love so much!), you'll always be my favorite dinner companions. And to my parents: I'll never stop saying thank you for everything you've given me. I love you both so much.

Guy, Joy, and Rae—this book is dedicated to you, because you three and your dad make my world go round. My biggest hope in life is that you all find the passions that make you feel alive, and I'm really grateful that I get to role-model that to you with my career while still aiming to be as good a mom as I can be to you. (And Guy—thank you for being my original *15 Minute Meal* companion during COVID lockdown. Have I done these acknowledgments properly and given you the extra shout-out you asked for? Ha!)

To Daniel: I love you (even if you'd usually rather order in). Thanks for being my person.

ABOUT THE AUTHOR

Ali Rosen is the Emmy and James Beard Award nominated host of *Potluck with Ali Rosen* on NYC Life. She is the author of the bestselling Amazon Editor's pick *Modern Freezer Meals* and *Bring It!*. She has been featured on shows like the *Today Show*, *Rachael Ray*, and *Food Network Kitchen*, and has written for publications including *Bon Appetit*, the *Washington Post* and *New York Magazine*. Aside from her work in food, she also has a novel, *Recipe for Second Chances*.

She is originally from Charleston, SC, but now lives in New York City with her husband and three kids. You can usually find her at the Union Square Greenmarket if she is not in her kitchen. But if you want to connect with her online, go to ali-rosen.com or find her on Instagram at @Ali_Rosen.

INDEX

A

M

N

O

P

V

Vinegar 24, 105, 181

  balsamic 37, 41, 190
  cider 38, 42, 54, 60, 85, 97, 148, 152
  red wine 154
  rice 85, 105, 158, 190
  sherry 45, 185
  white wine 85

W

wine 86

Y

yogurt 41, 63, 70, 142, 151, 180

Z

zucchini 75, 96, 154

Mango Publishing, established in 2014, publishes an eclectic list of books by diverse authors—both new and established voices—on topics ranging from business, personal growth, women's empowerment, LGBTQ studies, health, and spirituality to history, popular culture, time management, decluttering, lifestyle, mental wellness, aging, and sustainable living. We were named 2019 and 2020's #1 fastest growing independent publisher by Publishers Weekly. Our success is driven by our main goal, which is to publish high-quality books that will entertain readers as well as make a positive difference in their lives.

Our readers are our most important resource; we value your input, suggestions, and ideas. We'd love to hear from you—after all, we are publishing books for you!

Please stay in touch with us and follow us at:

Facebook: Mango Publishing
Twitter: @MangoPublishing
Instagram: @MangoPublishing
LinkedIn: Mango Publishing
Pinterest: Mango Publishing
Newsletter: mangopublishinggroup.com/newsletter

Join us on Mango's journey to reinvent publishing, one book at a time.